The Earth is flat.

The selective b... humans can weed ... from society.

Afri... ...eties

Hyst... ...olely affli... ...y be alle... ...tion.

Injecting monkeys' glands into humans encourages sexual rejuvenation.

Humans can be influenced by subliminal messaging.

All base metals can be turned into gold.

Tobacco can cure a variety of health problems.

Science

THEY GOT IT WRONG

Science

All the **Facts** That Turned Out to Be **Science Fiction**

Graeme Donald

Reader's
Digest

The Reader's Digest Association, Inc.
New York, NY / Montreal

Library of Congress Cataloging-in-Publication Data
Donald, Graeme.
  Science : all the facts that turned out to be science fiction / Graeme Donald.
    pages cm -- (They got it wrong)
  Summary: "The fascinating stories behind 50 scientific theories that were once regarded as facts but history proved were pure fictions.This is an innovative way into some truly zany bits of science and history that will surely fascinate readers. They Got It Wrong: Science tells the story behind 50 scientific theories that were once widely believed to be true, but history has since proved to be wrong, and the consequences it brought on at the time. Contents include: When the Earth was Flat, Tobacco can cure a variety of Health Problems, All Base metals can be turned into gold, how the physical measurements of the skull correlate to a person's personality, and more"-- Provided by publisher.
  Includes bibliographical references and index.
  ISBN 978-1-62145-009-2 (hardback) -- ISBN 978-1-62145-023-8 (adobe)
  1. Errors, Scientific--Miscellanea. 2. Pseudoscience--Miscellanea. 3. Science--History--Miscellanea. I. Title.
  Q172.5.E77D66 2013
  500--dc23
                            2012039974

ISBN 978-1-62145-009-2 (hardcover)
ISBN 978-1-62145-088-7 (paperback)

*For Rhona, as ever, and with very special thanks to Kath
"Kay-Dee" Davies, who selflessly moved heaven and earth to
give me the time to bring the manuscript in on time.*

CONTENTS

INTRODUCTION

∽◦∽

From ancient times to the modern day, science has strayed many times from the truth.

Often "discoveries" have been dictated by the constraints of contemporary thought. Take, for instance, the Ancient Greeks. They were so limited by their lack of knowledge of the human anatomy that they developed the theory that the body is made up of four humors, an idea that held sway until the march of scientific medicine in the nineteenth century (see page 170).

Other times false ideas were the result of pure folly, such as the seemingly innocuous development of phrenology—a concept eventually used to justify genocide in Rwanda in the late twentieth century. Sometimes scientific "facts" have been explored in an effort to lend false support to a hidden agenda, including the appropriation of the entirely spurious notion of subliminal messaging by politicians and the Christian Right. Despite the questionable nature of these ideas, *They Got It Wrong: Science* will highlight how man has been—and perhaps always will be—at the mercy of science.

Thankfully, not all the parts of science we got wrong have had devastating impacts; some of the examples in this book will raise a smile. Whether it's the alchemists' search for the philosopher's stone (the vehicle through which all base metals could be turned into gold), the somewhat surprising history of the vibrator, or the many proponents of the hollow earth theory, the annals of science are littered with strange people and their even stranger ideas.

What is perhaps most surprising is that some of science's most bogus ideas have been only recently relinquished. No matter how advanced today's medical and scientific thinking might be, who is to say that in one hundred years' time a book similar to this one won't be ridiculing today's wisdom?

The physical measurements of the skull correlate to a person's personality.

The majority of the scientific frivolities of previous centuries inflicted little or no real harm during their reign and evaporated without much trace in the light of new discoveries. Unfortunately, the same cannot be said for the pseudoscience of phrenology, which caused wide-ranging injustices and misery in its time and, most damaging of all, reached out from its grave to promote genocide at the close of the twentieth century.

THE GALL OF IT

The father of phrenology was the German physician Franz Joseph Gall (1758–1828), a product of the University of Vienna, an institution that served as a breeding ground for several other spurious notions about the human race (see box on page 15). Gall developed the theory that the human brain is comprised of twenty-seven distinct zones, each of which is a wholly separate and autonomous organ with individual responsibility for certain functions, characteristics, and predispositions.

The phrenological bust

MINI MYTH
Lessons in Idiocy

By 1925 the University of Vienna had become an intellectual hotbed of racist ideology. The most notorious and far-reaching of such notions was *Rassenpflege* — the quest for racial hygiene. Professor Otto Reche, director of the university's Department of Anthropology, was the most vocal proponent of such ideas, proclaiming, "*Rassenpflege* must be the basis for all domestic policy and at least a part of foreign policy as well."

The more an individual used one of the zones, or allowed themselves to be driven by the emotional or physical urges dictated by it, the larger that zone would become — similar to an overused muscle. In Gall's defense, his findings were not completely off the mark: It is now known that certain areas of the brain are linked to specific functions or temperament, and that some of these areas can become enlarged with mental exercise.

Had Franz Gall finalized his research at this point, no harm would have resulted. His error was in expanding the basic premise into the foundation stone of a sizeable edifice of speculation and assumption. By 1805 Gall had decided that the twenty-seven zones must be responsible for the lumps and bumps on the anterior of the skull, which they pressed against as they swelled with exertion.

REALITY CHECK
Brain Training

In March 2000, Professor Eleanor Maguire of University College London published the results of an extensive study she had conducted into the pattern of growth of the hippocampi in the brains of London taxi drivers. They were chosen because they were required to take "the knowledge," the formidable exam that demonstrates their ability to work out the best route between any two nominated points in the city. Professor Maguire deduced that the longer the driver had been working, the more pronounced the enlargement of the hippocampus.

LUNACY

Gall conducted exhaustive fingertip exploration on the skulls of murderers, burglars, and other categories of criminals and decided that there were sufficient significant similarities between them to establish a pattern. He also conducted similar explorations on the skulls of the insane and decided that their individual conditions were attributable to specific zonal malfunction. Again, in defense of Gall, some good did come of this thinking, as the insane were previously thought to be willfully so or possessed by the devil, and thus were beaten regularly. Such was the standing of phrenology that, almost overnight, the insane were for the first time regarded as genuinely ill and treated accordingly.

But this did not bode well for other people who, despite having previously led perfectly normal lives, happened to

Someone having their bumps felt

possess a few lumps and bumps similar to Gall's "scientifically proven" pattern, marking them out as potential murderers or lunatics. A few unfortunate souls found themselves locked up as a preventative measure. The public, too, became seduced by Gall's theories, which they picked up secondhand from the writings of celebrity converts including the Brontë sisters, Bram Stoker, and, most popular of all, the Sherlock Holmes yarns of Sir Arthur Conan Doyle. If it was good enough for Holmes, then it *had* to the right.

Companies incorporated phrenology in their personnel selection, with "experts" fondling the heads of prospective employees to ensure their clients were not about to hire a lunatic. In the courts, many defendants were imprisoned through convictions secured, in part, on the "expert witness" ramblings of professional phrenologists. But the cracks in Gall's edifice were already apparent by 1820 and by 1850 it lay in ruins—but only in the United Kingdom.

COMMITTING A FOWL

Phrenology was by this time deeply entrenched in the United States, mainly through the efforts of the Fowler brothers, Orson (1809–87) and Lorenzo (1811–96), who counted the likes of the American essayist Ralph Waldo Emerson (1803–82) and the inventor Thomas Edison (1847–1931) among their supporters. It would be unkind to brand the Fowlers as complete charlatans, but it should

From the March 1848 edition of the American Phrenological Journal, *edited by Orson Fowler*

be acknowledged that both had an eye for a fast buck—especially Lorenzo, who visited the UK in 1860 for a lecture tour that proved so lucrative he decided to stay.

While in London, Lorenzo established the Fowler Institute where, in 1872, author and humorist Mark Twain tried in vain to expose him. An inveterate prankster, Twain donned a lower-middle-class disguise and booked a reading during which Fowler, who showed little interest in his subject beyond the collection of the fee, identified a significant depression in Twain's skull that, he claimed, indicated a total lack of any sense of humor. The subject was also, in Fowler's professional opinion, lacking in any creative ability and best suited to mundane work of a clerical nature. Twain mumbled his humble thanks, paid, and left.

A month or so later, Twain rebooked under his own name and turned up in his trademark white suit, full of bravado and swagger. This time a much more obsequious Fowler lionized his celebrity client and, at the exact same spot on Twain's skull that had on the previous meeting presented a depression, there now appeared a "mountainous protrusion" consistent with the star's international reputation as a humorist. Twain paid his fee and left to publish the results. But nothing could stop the Fowler bandwagon. Lorenzo had by then set up a sizeable mail-order operation to provide the burgeoning craze for phrenology parties with all the necessary paraphernalia.

Any one of the iconic beige-colored phrenology busts complete with black markings (as seen in antique stores today) is likely to be one of Lorenzo's products. All harmless fun, perhaps, and certainly no more dangerous than the craze for Ouija sessions that was to follow. Fowler's other legacy has been the introduction into the English lexicon of expressions such as "high-brow," "low-brow," and anyone acting irrationally being told it is time they "had their bumps felt." But things were about to get worse—much worse.

A TURN FOR THE WORSE

The Treaty of Versailles (1919) turned the former German colony of Rwanda over to Belgian control. Proceedings took a dark turn when Belgium, too, fell foul to the phrenology craze, under the guiding hand of its leading proponent, Paul Bouts (1900–90). A priest-phrenologist who by the age of twenty-four was already a Belgian national celebrity, Bouts visited a variety of institutions throughout his homeland and measured inmates' heads with the aid of his self-designed instruments. He used his findings to make dubious pronouncements on who was "normal" and who was not.

To make matters worse, racial overtones began to creep in when Bouts's devices were used by the Belgian Colonial Office in Rwanda to decide on matters of racial superiority. After clamping a few heads in their mail-order calipers, the office pronounced the Tutsi to be racially superior to the Hutu, putting the one above the other in all matters and benefits. This set the stage for decades of racial inequality and led to the 1994 genocide in which Hutu extremists killed an estimated 500,000 to 1 million Tutsi and moderate Hutu.

Today, thankfully, the use of phrenology to segregate or degrade people in any way is widely condemned.

A battalion of marching soldiers can cause a suspension bridge to collapse.

In the nineteenth century the military was warned that all bodies of marching soldiers, from a single platoon to a full regiment, should always break step when passing over a bridge. The advice was reinforced by contemporary scientific discussions about the way in which all objects possess a natural frequency—the frequency with which something will vibrate once it has been set in motion. It was believed that if the repeated and synchronized step of the soldiers marching in cadence matched the natural frequency of the bridge they were crossing, catastrophe would inevitably ensue.

TROUBLED WATER

The notion was born of the Broughton Suspension Bridge disaster of April 12, 1831. Built in 1826 at the personal expense of wealthy Manchester inhabitant John Fitzgerald, the bridge spanned the River Irwell between Broughton and Pendleton in Lancashire. On the day in question, Lieutenant John Fitzgerald Jr. was leading seventy-four members of the 60th Rifle Corps back from exercise on the moors to the barracks in Salford. As they crossed the bridge, marching proudly in step, the structure began to collapse, and the entire column of men was tipped into the river. Fortunately the water was only approximately half a yard deep and the injuries suffered were minor.

Scientists were immediately consulted at the newly opened Manchester Mechanics' Institute, to which Fitzgerald had made considerable donations. They deduced that the collapse had been brought about by the resonance caused by the soldiers stamping along in unison. This conclusion brought some comfort to those who had invested in the suspension bridge—one of the earliest of its kind, the Broughton span was a matter of local pride, and those who had designed and built it did not wish to find themselves accused of incompetence, or worse. The military sent out an immediate instruction to all marching units, big or small, that soldiers were to break step and walk casually across any bridge for fear of bringing it crashing down.

MINI MYTHS
WELL, I NEVER!
POPULAR SCIENTIFIC IDEAS DEBUNKED

- There is no such thing as a centrifugal force.

- Heat does not rise but disperses itself equally and evenly throughout its environment.

- Stomach ulcers are not caused by stress or by spicy food but by a bacterium called *Helicobacter pylori*.

- A quantum leap does not denote a seismic step in progress, but a minute transitional change that occurs when matter shifts from one state to another without any discernible change in the process.

NUTS AND BOLTS

In reality, mechanical resonance, although a very real force, had nothing to do with the issue, nor had the marching troops. When the fuss died down and engineers unconnected to the bridge's patron investigated the site they found that one of the large bolts that secured one of the stay-chains to the ground anchor had snapped. It was also discovered that many of the other bolts that anchored the suspending chains were either cracked or bent, and the bolts used were three-year-old replacements of bolts that had failed before.

More pointed questioning revealed that the preeminent

structural engineer Eaton Hodgkinson (1789–1861) had ex-
pressed doubts about the strength of the chains and advised
they be tested before being installed on site; wise words
that went unheeded. Additionally, if the soldiers' marching
in step was the unforeseen harbinger of the bridge's doom,
why had it not collapsed when the troops had marched over
it on their way out to Kersal Moor? In effect, the bridge was
ready to fall down, and it just happened to do so under the
weight of the corps; marching in step had nothing to do with
it. It had been simple mechanical failure because the bridge
had been badly designed and built.

THE MYTH TAKES HOLD

Yet the myth that synchronized heavy footing could cause
a bridge to fall apart continued and was further reinforced
by the collapse of the Angers Suspension Bridge in France
on April 16, 1850. The bridge collapsed after two suspension cables snapped when a battalion of some 500 troops
marched across it amid a violent thunderstorm. A total of
226 soldiers lost their lives. Yet again marching-induced
mechanical resonance was blamed, despite the fact the
soldiers had been ordered to double space and break step.
In addition there was a significant troop presence in the
area and whole battalions routinely used the bridge, some
breaking step and others not. On April 16 two battalions
from the same regiment had crossed the bridge earlier in

The collapse of the Angers Suspension Bridge

the day, without incident. Again, corrosion problems were found at the anchor-points of the snapped cables. As in the case of the Broughton Suspension Bridge, the collapse of the Angers was the result of a simple mechanical failure.

REALITY CHECK
MILLENNIUM WOBBLE

In an article titled "London Bridge's Wobble and Sway" published in *Physics Today* in March 2010, physics professor Bernard J. Feldman challenged the argument that the wobble experienced on London's newly opened Millennium Bridge in June 2000 was the result of synchronized resonance. Key to his claim was that the walking frequency of pedestrians is double the lateral oscillation of bridges and thus unlikely to have any impact.

HIGH WINDS

The spectacular collapse of the Tacoma Narrows Suspension Bridge over the Puget Sound in Washington state in 1940 was automatically assumed to have been caused by wind-induced resonance. The bridge had already earned itself the nickname "Galloping Gertie" due to the way the deck bucked, even during construction. Despite this, the cataclysmic nature of the bridge's later collapse only caused one casualty: a spaniel named Tubby.

Even though the bridge was supposedly built to withstand 120 mph winds, the disaster happened in 40 mph winds. Nevertheless, wind-induced resonance was immediately blamed. The wind rushing past the bridge was thought to have created a stream of whirlwinds, the fluctuations of which matched the bridge's natural frequency. The vibrations then reached such a pitch the bridge was forced to collapse.

THE BACKLASH BEGINS

Today, talk of Gertie falling foul of mechanical or wind-induced resonance still abounds, but with a few exceptions. Robert H. Scanlan (1914–2001) wrote several papers that lambasted this misconception and, as the main consultant on the Golden Gate Bridge project, his comments came with some authority. Hailed internationally as the "father" of the study of the aerodynamics and aeroelasticity of such structures, Scanlan, along with other leading lights in the field, repeatedly poured cold water on the Tacoma resonance theory.

Professor P. Joseph McKenna and Professor Alan C. Lazer's article "Rock and Roll Bridge" leads a very convincing case against the Tacoma resonance theory. For them, resonance is a very precise entity. Using the shattering of glass as an example, McKenna and Lazer describe the unique circumstances needed for the forcing frequency to match the natural frequency of the object. Such "precise, steady conditions" are unlikely to have been in place during the powerful storm that hit the Tacoma Bridge. Rather, they attribute the bridge's demise to the different types of oscillation it experienced during the storm, which resulted in an extreme twisting of the roadway. It could also be noted that the pressure on the suspension cables as the Tacoma roadway lifted and fell violently in the wind would not have helped matters either.

Despite the unique circumstances of their individual demise, the collapsing of the Broughton, Angers, and Tacoma bridges had nothing to do with resonance theory. Yet the old errors of science do not always die that easily, which is why to this day troops will always break step on bridges, just in case there is anything in the old wives' tale.

MINI MYTH
HITTING A HIGH NOTE

The other great resonance myth is that glass can be shattered by the human voice. Scientists of the nineteenth century believed an opera singer could hit and hold a note long enough to shatter a drinking glass. Despite the number of ear-splitting salon demonstrations, something was amiss — the human voice simply is not powerful enough to shatter glass. But whichever trick was used — an accomplice with an air-pistol would not have been heard amid the racket — science was once again duped into extolling the power of resonance.

More recently, a famous television advertisement showed Ella Fitzgerald apparently pulling off a similar trick, but that too was rigged. The glass itself holds the secret: It has first to be "pinged" to reveal its own note of resonance; this must then be recorded and played back in the direction of the glass through loudspeakers until the glass shatters. The human voice lacks the necessary power — volume holds the key.

All base metals can be turned into gold.

The origin of the word "alchemy" is thought by some to be derived from the Arabic *al-Khemia*, meaning the (land of the) Black Earth, which is an ancient epithet of Egypt. Europe's introduction to alchemy—which is the father of modern chemistry—occurred during the eleventh century when it was introduced to Spain by the Moors. Aside from a few grand principles (including plans to discover the secrets to eternal life) alchemy's prime goal was the search for the "philosopher's stone"—the vehicle through which base metals could be turned into gold. This quest is what the "science" of alchemy is remembered for most.

ELEMENTARY MATTERS

The basis of alchemy was the Aristotelian concept that all matter was alike—a cabbage and a brick are comprised of exactly the same substances, they just assumed a different form and inspirational spirit. In order to turn a cabbage into a brick, for example—or a lump of lead into gold—a person needed to first identify the "spirit" of the cabbage or the brick and imbue the one with the other.

Although alchemists acknowledged the four classical elements of earth, fire, water, and air, they regarded them as different manifestations of the same, singular matter. If a person were to heat water, for example, it would become air; if the air was chilled, water appeared. These natural phenomena were seen by the alchemists as validations of their basic premise.

In alchemists' circles, the search for the philosopher's stone was termed the "Magnum Opus," a term now applied to a person's greatest work. But the question that remains unanswered is: Why were so many bright people duped into believing such an absurd principle? And they seemed not to realize that if lead could be turned so easily into gold, then the price would drop out of the gold market and gold would become as cheap as, well, lead. But greed, it seems, blinded all—medieval Europe teemed with charlatan alchemists who happily ripped off wealthy and avaricious nobles, all too eager to part with their money after witnessing a few shabby tricks dressed up to look like miracles.

An artistic representation of the philosopher's stone

CELEBRITY CONVERTS

Not all alchemists were focused exclusively on fleecing the gullible; some very bright minds joined the quest for the key to all matter and made significant contributions to science and medicine along the way. The alchemist Paracelsus (1493–1541) was the first to identify and name zinc (from the old German word "zinke" for "pointed," based on the pointed appearance of its crystals after smelting). He also invented laudanum, an alcoholic solution that contained morphine and was later guzzled enthusiastically by Victorian ladies until over-the-counter sales of opium products became illegal in 1920 (see page 101).

The lure of alchemy was strong, and in Paracelsus's time—as well as for a couple centuries after—the dividing line between the ethical strands of alchemy and mainstream science was blurred. Sir Isaac Newton (1642–1727), one of the science world's most influential pioneers, and John Dee (1527–c. 1608), consultant to Queen Elizabeth I, both dabbled on the dark side.

Not all experiments ended well. The celebrated alchemist Dr. Faustus (1480–1540), having made countless enemies in the ranks of the clergy—a few of whom he managed to poison with his alchemic remedies—blew himself to smithereens while he experimented with glycerin and acids in his search for the "Water of Life." If the acid Dr. Faustus had used was nitric acid then it is little wonder there was nothing left of him: He may have been 200 years ahead of the invention of nitroglycerine, a highly explosive liquid that has since been used in the production of dynamite. Regardless, the church explained that the absence of bodily remains was result of the devil's work.

An image from Michael Maier's alchemical emblem book Atalanta Fugiens. *Gold and silver (the sun and the moon) are shown to be in conjunction.*

MINI MYTHS
WELL, I NEVER!
POPULAR SCIENTIFIC IDEAS DEBUNKED

- There is no such thing as a tongue map: sweet, sour, salt, and other flavors can be detected all over the organ.

- It is your sense of smell that you lose with a cold, not your sense of taste.

- "Sixth sense" is a silly expression because humans actually possess nineteen senses.

RICH EXPERIMENTATION

If Faustus had discovered nitroglycerine, if only for a fraction of the second before it killed him, he was not the only alchemist to be ahead of the game of traditional science. But the sinister reputation of the art clouded alchemists' discoveries with suspicion and papal objections, subsequently holding back scientific development. The basic principle held that if it came out of an alchemist's workshop, then it was likely the work of the devil himself.

One such pioneer whose discoveries were disregarded was the Polish alchemist Michael Sendivogius (1566–1636), who produced oxygen by heating nitrous almost 200 years before theologian Joseph Priestley (1733–1804) was acclaimed for the "discovery" of the same in 1774. Sendivogius successfully managed to share his knowledge with the Dutch alchemist Cornelis Drebbel (1572–1633), who put it to great and advanced practical use. In London in 1620, Drebbel built the first dirigible submarine, capable of carrying sixteen people. Drebbel had discovered that by burning potassium nitrate or sodium nitrate he could not only produce oxygen, but the process also transmuted the nitrates to an oxide or hydroxide that absorbed the build-up of carbon dioxide. Thus, he, too, found himself 300 years ahead of his time by producing a crude but effective re-breathing system. The submarine was tested with a full crew in the Thames in front of James I and the British navy. It stayed submerged for more than three hours as it traveled up and down the river at a depth of approximately five yards. But again whispers of satanic involvement abounded, and the navy was deprived of functioning submarines for war purposes.

Heading into the laboratory: (a) copper still; (b) still head; (c) cooling medium; (d) condensing tube; (e) receiver

BAD REPUTATION

Despite such pioneering discoveries, it was the charlatans who grabbed the limelight and dragged the name of alchemy through the mud. The court of the Habsburgs, one of the most important European dynasties, found itself vulnerable to alchemy's dark side. Holy Roman Emperor Ferdinand III (1608–57) was duped into believing he had witnessed the creation of a nugget of gold. He heaped a fortune on the Austrian alchemist Johann Richthausen, who promptly made off with the proceeds. Then Leopold I (1640–1705) was similarly hoodwinked, and it fell to the wiser Empress Maria Theresa (1717–80) to ban all attempts of transmutation throughout her realm.

But now it seems that the worst of alchemy's practitioners may have been on to something after all. Today, particle accelerators, like the Large Hadron Collider on the Franco-Swiss border, routinely transmute a variety of elements by knocking free neutrons and protons from one element or by bombarding an element with protons from another. So, while transmutation by chemical means may well be impossible, it is not so in the realm of physics. In 1972, Soviet physicists at the research facility on the shores of Lake Baikal in Siberia reported that, on a routine inspection, the lead lining of the deflector shields in an experimental reactor had turned to gold. Naturally, this was questioned by a skeptical West until Glenn Seaborg, Nobel

Laureate for Chemistry, managed to achieve the same result at the University of California in 1980.

Under the arm of nuclear physics, Seaborg successfully transformed several thousand atoms of lead and bismuth into gold by removing certain neutrons and protons from the sample. Although this may go some way to vindicate the notions of the early alchemists, the process costs many thousand times what gold is worth when it is mined in the traditional way, so the gold market can rest easy for at least a little while longer.

Hysteria is a condition that solely afflicts women, and it can only be alleviated by genital stimulation.

An etymological sister of the word hysterectomy, *hysteria* is derived from the Greek *hustera*, meaning womb. The condition was, from ancient times and until quite recently, believed in medical circles to be the exclusive province of women and caused by an imbalance in their wombs or vaginas. Today experts recognize that the impetus for this diagnosis was social rather than medical. Any woman who was opinionated, assertive, or unable to stick to the genteel code of Victorian female behavior might be labeled as having "hysteria." The somewhat far-fetched notion was rendered more farcical by the suggested treatment for the condition that was accepted medical practice until well into the twentieth century. The acceptance of these methods in the annals of medicine led indirectly to the development of the vibrating sex-toy industry.

PAROXYSMS OF JOY

In 1563, the Dutch physician Pieter van Foreest (1521–97) concurred with the centuries-old remedy for "hysteria," or "womb disease," when he wrote the following in his published collection of medical observation:

> When these symptoms indicate, we think it necessary to ask a midwife to assist, so that she can massage the genitalia with one finger inside, using oil of lilies, musk root, crocus, or similar. And in this way the afflicted woman can be aroused to the paroxysm. This kind of stimulation with the finger is recommended by Galen and Avicenna, among others, most especially for widows, those who live chaste lives, and female religious, as Gradus proposes; it is less often recommended for very young women, public women, or married women, for whom it is a better remedy to engage in intercourse with their spouses.

In other words, if a woman got a bit irritable or argumentative, all she needed was genital stimulation, by one means or another. This attitude to the fairer sex pervaded throughout the centuries, and in Victorian times, many men simply did not take women seriously and did not even consider them as sexual creatures capable of orgasm. Much of the medical profession was no better informed.

Following the ancient advice, Victorian doctors advocated genital massage for any woman prone to "the vapors," a collective term used to describe symptoms that included tiredness, shortness of breath, insomnia, lack of appetite, general irritability, or simply disagreeing with one's husband. The archives are full of doctors bemoaning the time spent inducing physician-assisted "paroxysm," which technically means spasm, because certain uncooperative patients took their time reaching the conclusion.

Extraordinarily, no member of the medical community realized these paroxysms were a female orgasm—apart perhaps from the patients, who for the most part proclaimed themselves to feel much better after their first treatment and immediately agreed to join the ongoing program. Consequently, gynecological massage clinics—they would be called something quite different today—sprang up all over Europe and America.

SUPPLY AND DEMAND

As the demand for such treatments grew to quite alarming proportions, doctors complained of sore fingers and wrists, quickly joining the ranks of the first acknowledged victims of repetitive strain injury (RSI). The Swiss found the solution in a handheld clockwork device that thumped adequately well. But the silly things kept running out of power just as the patients showed signs of impending paroxysm—

shortness of breath, flushing of the skin around the neck and treatment area, and sometimes grunting noises. (One can only assume not one single nineteenth-century doctor's wife enjoyed a happy sex life, because these professionals failed to recognize the patients' responses for what they really were.)

Next on the list, and slightly more successful, was hydro-percussion, which used water-jets aimed at the clitoris and brought about rapid and intense paroxysms. Unsurprisingly, it was a hit among patients, and doctors were forced to conclude that hydro-percussion induced a more powerful paroxysm, which was thus all the better for the patient. Demand increased exponentially.

However, the cost of the equipment and the fact that a room set up for such treatment was of little use for anything else put hydro-percussion out of the hands of all but the wealthiest physicians and patients. So in came the recently revived spa clinics, already in the aqua-treatment business, where doctors set up discreet centers where ladies flocked to "take the waters" twice daily for one week.

MACHINE TAKES OVER

Meanwhile, in 1868 Dr. George Taylor of New York, tired of relieving a woman's hysteria by hand — the strain brought on by the number of paroxysms he was required to induce meant he could no longer hold his golf clubs properly — devised a new solution: a treatment table that incorporated

MINI MYTH
A Spring in Her Step

The famous French physician Henri Scoutetten's notes from 1843 on hydro-percussion as a remedy for "female pelvic congestion" revealed why the practice had become so popular:

> The first impression produced by the jet of water is painful, but soon the effect of the percussion, the reaction of the organism to the cold, which causes the skin to flush, and the re-establishment of equilibrium all create so agreeable a sensation that it is necessary to take precautions that they do not go beyond the prescribed time, which is usually four or five minutes. After the douche, the patient dries herself off, refastens her corset, and returns with a brisk step to her room.

a steam-driven vulvar agitator that pounded away from below a durable rubber membrane.

It was an immediate hit within the medical profession. Simple to use and with minimal effort involved, all the physician had to do was to instruct his patient to lie facedown on the table with her "treatment area" positioned over the central aperture. He then fired up the device and asked the patient to make whatever minor adjustments in her position she felt necessary to the successful conclusion of the treatment. But problems with Taylor's table soon arose: It

Somewhat cumbersome:
the vibrator and the treatment table

was large and cumbersome, not to mention noisy, and the recipients of its attentions found it all a bit impersonal. Apparently most preferred the personal touch.

GRANVILLE'S HAMMER

The solution came in 1880 when Britain's Dr. Joseph Mortimer Granville (1833–1900) designed and patented the world's first handheld electric vibrator for clinical use. He liked to call it his "percussor," but everyone else, much to the doctor's chagrin, coined it "Granville's Hammer."

In profile the percussor resembled a cross between a hair dryer and a tool a mechanic might use to remove wheel nuts. It could be fitted with a variety of differently shaped rubber heads and was suspended from a moveable platform when not in use. And best of all, the patients loved it—they flocked to be percussed, again and again.

Although Granville himself never used it, stating in his paper "Nerve-Vibration and Excitation as Agents in the Treatment of Functional Disorder and Organic Disease" (1883): "I have never yet percussed a female patient. . . . I have avoided, and shall continue to avoid the treatment of women by percussion, simply because I do not wish to be hoodwinked, and help to mislead others, by the vagaries of the hysterical state."

In 1902 the American market responded to Granville's invention with a less industrial-looking unit for "self-treatment," sounding the death knell for a majority of the discreet gynecological massage parlors and for the medical "pelvic percussing" market. First marketed by the still-extant domestic appliance company Hamilton Beach, the handheld vibrator was the fifth domestic appliance to be electrified, after the fan, the kettle, the sewing machine, and the pop-up toaster.

On the move: the portable vibrator

A QUIVERING SUCCESS

And there was gold in them there thrills! Demand was enormous. Widely advertised in respectable publications ranging from the *Sears-Roebuck Catalogue* to the suitably named *Woman's Home Companion*, a whole variety of vibrator models were soon available to suit every budget. These ranged in power from approximately 1,000 pulses a minute on the cheap-and-cheerful models to the top-of-the-range models, including the much eulogized Chattanooga, which cost approximately $200 and delivered an eye-watering 8,000 pulses a minute.

The Chattanooga was a free-standing device, roughly 1 yard in height, with a maneuverable "action arm" that could be lowered to a person laying down, giving them access to the business end of the device, which was tipped with something resembling a large suppository. Now stripped of their highly lucrative onanistic revenue stream, high-profile doctors fell over one another in the rush to market their own such devices. And

The Chattanooga

Health for Women could not recommend them enough as the only resort for those suffering from "pelvic congestion," who would soon find that "all the pleasures of youth which will once again throb within you."

NAUGHTY BUT NICE

Thousands of American and European women did indeed throb away to their hearts' content, while the menfolk twirled their waxed moustaches and continued to mutter about "women's problems." It may strike the modern reader as incredible that until only the last century thousands of ladies were routinely masturbated by doctors, while their husbands remained oblivious. But then most men, including doctors, were fairly ignorant of female sexuality. Men enjoyed sex and women tolerated it—that was the natural order of things. It is little wonder, therefore, that women popped out for the odd physician-assisted paroxysm, or invested in a Chattanooga "choo-choo" of their own.

By the 1920s medical masturbation had ceased to be prescribed, and ladies' percussers had become handheld, battery-powered devices, ultimately stripped of their thin veneer of respectability when they made regular appearances in the growing sex-film industry. And finally, in 1952, "hysteria," along with all its attendant symptoms, was removed from all official lists of recognized medical conditions.

MINI MYTH
SERIOUS BUSINESS

All this percussing was absolutely not regarded as a furtive and seedy sideline of medicine. *The Merck Manual*, still a respected doctors' guide, listed in its first edition of the twentieth century "female hysteria" as a recognized condition. "Pelvic massage," by manual or mechanical means, was recommended as the only effective treatment. And, as proof that no individual, not even at the beginning of the twentieth century, thought there might be a sexual angle to all this percussing, the same manual suggested sulfuric acid should be used to remove sensation from the clitoris of any woman who showed excessive interest in or derived "too much pleasure" from sexual arousal.

Tobacco can cure a variety of health problems.

Tobacco takes its name from an early Caribbean word for a cigar (hence the name given to the cigar-shaped island Tobago) and was first brought to Europe from the Americas in or around 1518 by the Spanish—not, as myth would have it, by Sir Walter Raleigh. When tobacco was first introduced to the West it was welcomed as a medicinal miracle that could cure much of that which ails man.

A CURE-ALL

The noxious weed was immediately touted as a wondrous herbal remedy by its importers. They regaled the Spanish and Portuguese courts with tales of the native suppliers eulogizing the benefits of tobacco smoke enemas, in particular. Although it seems a not insignificant detail was lost in translation: The native tobacco vendors in fact only used tobacco remedies to cure constipation in their horses. But with the absence of this technicality, Europeans enthusiastically adopted the practice. Smoke-enema treatments, at the time referred to as "glysters," became very popular across much of the continent and would remain so until the mid-nineteenth century.

The case for the many benefits of tobacco was significantly buoyed by the findings of the Spanish physician and botanist Nicolás Monardes (1493–1588). His book on its use in the treatment of a whole host of conditions, ranging from constipation to epilepsy, was published in three parts from 1565 to 1574. As a consequence of Monardes's

REALITY CHECK
THE FIRST SMOKING BAN

It may come as something of a surprise for anti-tobacco campaigners to learn, but Adolf Hitler was, in fact, the main driving force behind the first-ever national anti-smoking program. After Nazi doctors discovered the first proof of a link between smoking and lung cancer, and the risk smoking posed to unborn children, Hitler's regime implemented a series of strategies aimed at reducing tobacco consumption.

It was Nazi Germany that banned smoking on public transportation, in air-raid shelters, and in several public buildings and restaurants, as well as forbidding advertising that presented smoking in a positive light. Smoking was not allowed in the Luftwaffe, and SS officers were banned from lighting up while on duty.

discoveries, smoke blowing was then used to help cure a range of ills — those afflicted by earaches had tobacco smoke blown in their ears; those with sinus problems received smoke up the nose; and those with gastrointestinal problems had smoke blown in them by another route altogether.

Hard as it may be to contemplate today, from the early sixteenth century until the mid-nineteenth century, the great and the good lined up to have smoke pumped up their rear ends by a contraption that looked like a cross between a pair of fireside bellows and an incense burner. While the common man preferred to take in his tobacco smoke in a more conventional manner, those who could afford it submitted themselves to smoke enemas with relish. Despite the indignity of the procedure, the trend spawned a veritable industry, complete with its own hierarchy. On the bottom rung were the "lemonaders," whose unenviable duty it was to clean out the waiting patient with lemonade before the more highly regarded "fumier" came in to do his job.

THE PROOF IS IN THE PUFFING

An incident in Oxford in December 1650 further cemented the idea that the smoke enema held supposedly miraculous powers. A young servant-girl called Anne Greene was wrongly accused and convicted of the murder of her own child, which had in fact been stillborn. Hanged before the obligatory yelling mob, Greene's body was taken down and carted away for dissection by would-be surgeons. During the procedure someone in the morgue thought they detected a slight twitch of Greene's fingers, so she was immediately administered a smoke enema in an attempt to revive her. It

Brace yourself: the tools of the trade

was a success—she sat up in startled confusion and received a full pardon. Greene went on to become a living advertisement for the apparently wondrous powers of the treatment.

While the smoke enema treatment held sway, it was widely respected in the canon of accepted medicine. In 1774, the Society for the Recovery of Persons Apparently Drowned was formed, aimed at promoting lifesaving intervention in the case of drowning. The society used the money received from public donations to install smoke enema huts along the London reaches of the Thames and at strategic points on the city's larger lakes. Inspired by Anne Greene, the society wanted to provide people with a fail-safe method of either establishing death or of resuscitating victims of near drowning. The society did in fact enjoy numerous successes and, from such unlikely beginnings, it evolved into the present-day Royal Humane Society.

MINI MYTH
ALL THAT GLISTERS . . .

Despite their surge in popularity, smoke enema treatments were not universally embraced. Shakespeare's "all that glisters is not gold" from *The Merchant of Venice* is said by some to be a pun based on the practice.

And the treatment did not catch on so well in America. The phrase "to blow smoke up someone's ass," which refers to an attempted con or deception, was coined in response to the questionable credibility of smoke enemas.

PURE POISON

Anal fumigation went into decline in the early nineteenth century as scientific research began to reveal tobacco's poisonous qualities. The English physiologist and surgeon Sir Benjamin Brodie provided the most significant research in this area when he discovered that nicotine, the principal component of tobacco, can interfere with blood circulation. Nevertheless, physicians still used tobacco smoke to treat cholera. No matter how improbable this sounds, it must be remembered that this was before the broad acceptance of germ theory, and all disease was thought to be transmitted by foul smells (malaria literally translates to "bad air"; see page 113). Free tobacco was issued following every outbreak of cholera, with all recipients, including children, required to puff away to create a fog to fight off the cholera "fumes."

MINI MYTH
DEARLY DEPARTED

The notoriety of Greene's enema also gave rise to the habit within wealthy circles of pumping the recently departed with smoke, "just to make sure"—even in death there was no escaping the smoking glyster. In the early nineteenth century, when that practice had fallen from grace, those fearful of being buried alive could have a bell-string installed in the coffin to alert graveyard attendants to their predicament.

A device for administering smoke enemas

COLONICS CATCH ON

Despite the treatment's general decline by the mid-nineteenth century, smoke enemas had a lasting legacy—as the fumiers disappeared, the lowly lemonaders rose to take their place. People had grown used to, and even obsessed with, things being shoved up their backsides, and they seem to have decided that even if the smoke had to go, why not stick with the lemonade wash. Although there is evidence to suggest the Ancient Egyptians and Greeks favored such "hygiene," this was the beginning of the still-continuing and rather questionable trend for colonic irrigation—as championed by the late Princess of Wales, who apparently had a thrice weekly "royal flush," each of which involved a staggering twelve gallons of sterilized mineral water.

As a consequence of a sixteenth-century translator's inattention to detail, there exists today a multibillion-dollar industry of colonic irrigation clinics enjoyed by the modern counterparts of the smoke enema devotees. The administrators of the smoke enema could be excused for not knowing any better; they actually thought they were administering a valid treatment. The same, however, cannot be said for the modern-day irrigation lobby, which has managed to convince its patients that we are all being slowly poisoned by impacted fecal matter sticking to the inside of the large intestine.

No autopsy performed since records began has ever found evidence to support this, and the pointless and, it could be argued, dangerous practice of irrigation can cause side effects ranging from amoebic infection to internal perforations and heart failure.

In the wake of the smoke

Injecting monkeys' glands into humans encourages sexual rejuvenation.

For centuries people, or rather men, have been searching for substances that will render women so sexually aroused that they will welcome their advances and reawaken the most listless loins. Until the invention of Viagra (although technically not an aphrodisiac) in the late twentieth century, the most famous sexual stimulant was Spanish Fly. Prepared from the wing-sheaths of the blister beetle, this aphrodisiac has been used and abused by the torpid and lusty since Roman times.

How its reputation has endured, however, is a mystery, as the closest to any aphrodisiac effect it engenders is irritation of the urinary tract, with other side effects ranging from vomiting, diarrhea, and permanent damage to the kidneys to cardiac arrhythmia and death. Far from lighting people's fires, Spanish Fly would have put a damper on any Roman orgy; and yet it is still touted in liquid and tablet form on the Internet today for those who like to live dangerously—or not at all.

*A helping hand: an aphrodisiac
containing Spanish Fly*

FOOD OF LOVE

Over the centuries, various foods have enjoyed transient
notoriety for their supposed aphrodisiac effects. Sixteenth-
century Spanish explorers were entranced by the pendu-
lous avocado fruits of Mexico, especially when they were
told *avocado* meant "testicle" in the local tongue. The amo-
rous conquistadores immediately began shipping the fruits
home, where they would be turned into a paste for foolish
old men to apply to their genitals while sitting out in the
sun. Naturally the crushed avocados failed to have the de-
sired effect, but the Mexicans, it seems, derived no end of
amusement from tales of such antics.

MINI MYTH
THE HUMBLE TOMATO

The tomato once enjoyed extended infamy as a potent aphrodisiac. The fruit was introduced to Europe by the Moors, which prompted the French to call it *pomme de Moor*. The English misheard this as *pomme d'amour*, or love apple, and leaped to the inevitable conclusion. The medieval church mounted a counterattack by suggesting the fruit was in fact poisonous.

Because the tomato plant resembles a deadly nightshade (to which it is in fact related), notions of the fruit's so-called toxicity became enshrined in medical lore. The idea became cemented in the sixteenth-century mind with the publication of John Gerard's *Herball* (1597), which condemned the plant for generations to come. Long after the Church had moved on to other concerns, the medical profession was still firmly of the opinion that anyone who ate two or three tomatoes would suffer instant death. It was not until the early to mid-eighteenth century that this idea was on the whole disproved following simple experimentation on behalf of thrill-seekers.

Americans remained convinced of the tomato's toxicity until the early nineteenth century, when, according to legend, Colonel Robert Gibbon Johnson stood on the steps of the Old Courthouse of Salem on September 26, 1820, and ate a basketful before an astonished crowd.

TESTICLE TREATMENT

The quest for sexual rejuvenation continued, soon to be appropriated by the far-from-ethical Russian-born French surgeon Serge Voronoff (1866–1951), who, along with his compatriot Ilya Ivanov (see page 133), may have been responsible for the deaths of millions of people worldwide.

In 1889, while conducting pioneering research into methods of curbing the aging process, Voronoff began to practice his methods on himself, injecting his body with extracts from ground-up dog and guinea pig testicles. The effects were barely perceptible, so Voronoff moved on to glandular tissue transplants of the same substance and published papers eulogizing it as the way forward in the fight against everything from flagging desire to schizophrenia. The international press and the European and American medical profession naively accepted Voronoff's findings without ever asking him for corroborative evidence.

In early 1920 Voronoff began transplanting the testes of executed criminals into the gullible who had cash to spare. When supply failed to keep up with demand, he began using monkey testicles, grafting thin slices of the glands into the scrotums of the rich and famous. By 1922, monkey gland treatment was the talk of the medical profession. Voronoff grew rich, not only from the operations he conducted on the likes of Kemal Atatürk, the first president of the Republic of Turkey, and other heads of state, but also from the income he generated by teaching other doctors and surgeons to expand his folly across the rest of Europe and America.

In 1923 more than 700 high-status delegates of the International Congress of Surgeons came from all over Europe and America to laud Voronoff at a conference in London and to hail him as the father of rejuvenation. However, no person in attendance seemed to notice that the master himself looked a trifle aged and balding; or if they did, no one had the courage to cry, "Physician, heal thyself!"

REALITY CHECK
IT FELT LIKE A GOOD IDEA AT THE TIME

In the late 1780s bunnies were introduced to Australia. The fox was introduced 100 years later to deal with the rabbits' expanding population—but instead of eating the rabbits, the foxes preferred to eat the sheep. Eventually, in the 1950s the bunny-killing virus myxomatosis was unleashed to undo what should never have been done in the first place.

DISAPPOINTING RESULTS

By 1930 Voronoff had packed monkey genitals into the scrotums of more than 500 wealthy patients in France alone, but he would soon overplay his hand. Diversifying into the female market, Voronoff began transplanting monkey ovaries into women who feared the onset of age. At first, women flocked to his surgery door as the carrot of lasting allure proved too strong to resist. The results were disappointing. None of Voronoff's female patients saw any discernible slow down in their natural aging. To make matters worse, many of the men Voronoff had treated in the early 1920s began to die in large numbers; dark mutterings of disillusionment and dissent grew louder.

It then became public that Voronoff had transplanted a human ovary into a female monkey and had inseminated it with human sperm. This was a step too far for his now less-than-adoring public. The hitherto sycophantic medical profession also found itself getting twitchy, and it started to shine the harsh light of skepticism, which should have been directed long before, on to Voronoff's work and claims.

By the close of the 1930s, not only were most of Voronoff's early patients six feet under—none having fathered broods of children late in life, nor having lived past any conventional age—but testosterone had been synthesized, enabling direct-injection comparison tests to be conducted. As these tests were progressing, Voronoff, knowing full well what the results would be, quietly prepared for a life of opulent retirement in Switzerland.

As Voronoff expected, none of the experiments he had claimed to have conducted on the rejuvenation of farmyard animals could be replicated. The whole charade might have been quite amusing were it not for one troublesome detail. The modern scourge of HIV is not a disease of the 1980s (see page 136) but one that first arose in the late 1920s when SIV, the simian equivalent, somehow jumped the species barrier. Not surprisingly, there are many today who work and research in that field of medicine who consider the transplanting of monkey reproductive organs into assorted humans to have been a possible vector.

The selective breeding of humans can weed out the weak from society.

Charles Darwin (1809–82) could never have foreseen the long-term ramifications of his published works. In the short term the fallout was bad enough. Denounced by members of the church who, along with other ill-informed antagonists, had not even read his work properly, Darwin was rebuked for proclaiming man is the descendant of monkeys. In reality, he had not proposed anything of the sort. In the long term, the effects were far more devastating. "Survival of the fittest," a phrase attributed to Darwin, was later used by tyrannical elements in justification of, among other oppressive policies, the new "science" of eugenics. Darwin did not invent the expression; and the man who *had* coined the phrase, the English biologist, philosopher, and sociologist Herbert Spencer (1820–1903), had in fact intended it to mean those creatures best fitted to their environment, be they weak *or* strong.

EUGENICS IS BORN

The most questionable scientific idea based on Darwin's work arose when his own cousin, Francis Galton (1822–1911) — the man who championed the use of fingerprints in criminal detection — used Darwin's work as the basis for eugenics. Derived from the Greek *eugenes* (of noble race or birth), eugenics advocated controlled breeding in an attempt to increase the chances of desirable characteristics in offspring.

Like many intellectuals, Darwin spoke before considering the repercussions. In his *The Descent of Man, and Selection in Relation to Sex* (1882) he mused on how medical and scientific advances had meant that the weaker and less productive of our species were artificially propped up to allow them to survive and breed; a harsher environment would naturally cull such parasites. At his most incendiary, Darwin suggested:

> Thus the weaker members of civilized societies propagate their kind. . . . No one who has attended to the breeding of domestic animals will doubt that this must be highly injurious to the race of man . . . but there appears to be at least one check in steady action, namely that the weaker and inferior members of society do not marry so freely as the sound; and this check might be indefinitely increased by the weak in body or mind refraining from marriage, though this is more to be hoped for than expected.

Within a matter of months of reading his cousin's book
Galton had formulated his own take on the future of humanity. British society—and indeed the entire world—would
benefit enormously if all such dead wood was eliminated.
His *Inquiries into Human Faculty and Its Development* (1883)
first coined the term *eugenics*.

Eugenics makes the world go 'round:
the front cover of America's satirical
Puck *magazine, June 1913*

GENETICS HOLDS THE KEY

It all made perfect sense: Breeding kennels always match the strongest and the smartest dog with the smartest and the best bitch, and the equine bloodstock lines had been running on the same principles for centuries. New discoveries in the science of genetics further helped Galton's case. Gregor Mendel's experiments on pea patches (see box on facing page) led to an understanding of how heredity works. When Mendel crossed pea plants with defined but opposite characteristics—for example, a long and a short stem—the result was not an average of the two heights, but a tall plant. In an outright challenge to contemporary scientific thought that believed offspring inherited a blend of their parents' characteristics, Mendel's discoveries concluded that inherited characteristics can be passed on to offspring unaltered, with the strongest predominating. Galton's eugenics applied Mendel's findings to the human race: Why not selectively breed together the very best and in the process weed out the worst of the species from the gene pool?

While Galton did not suggest that extant individuals deemed to be defective should be eliminated, he did suggest they be sterilized in order to prevent them from propagating any more of their kind. Nobility of spirit, intelligence, and artistic talent were, he decided, all inherited traits, as were fecklessness, imbecility, promiscuity, drunkenness, and criminality. To him, it would be no different to the selective breeding of dogs or thoroughbreds. Galton promised that within the span of a few generations crime and antisocial behavior would be a thing of the past and Britain would be left teeming with pleasant people who bore increasingly talented offspring.

REALITY CHECK
THE FATHER OF GENETICS

The Abbot of the Augustine Abbey of St. Thomas at Brno, Gregor Mendel (1822–84), conducted research into peas grown in the abbey grounds, and his findings awarded him the posthumous recognition as the founder of genetics. Mendel conducted his experiments between 1856 and 1863, and the results led him to devise his two laws of inheritance.

The first law (The Law of Segregation) stated that an individual possesses two alleles (a different form of a gene) for any given trait, one of which is passed on from the mother, the second from the father; whichever of these two alleles is dominant determines the character of the offspring. The second law (The Law of Independent Assortment) stated that separate genes for separate traits are passed on independently of one another. When Mendel published his results in 1866 they were met with derision. It was not until the turn of the century that the "Father of Genetics" was rediscovered.

GALTON'S SUPPORTERS

Many of the great and good of Europe and America flocked eagerly to follow Galton's banner. Notable figures including Winston Churchill and Theodore Roosevelt were open and ardent supporters of Galton's movement, as were birth control activists Marie Stopes and Margaret Sanger. Economists such as John Maynard Keynes and Sidney Webb, the cofounder of the London School of Economics, saw the financial sense of a society unfettered by the financial burden of supporting an ever-increasing number of unproductive dependants. The American proponent of moral and edible fiber, John Harvey Kellogg, was also in support of anything that improved the purity of the species. Indeed, his most famous product was initially intended to be an antimasturbation measure—a plain diet, so Kellogg thought, would dampen passionate thoughts.

LEFT-WING SUPPORT

Many today dismiss the eugenics bandwagon as an exclusively right-wing vehicle, but this was far from the case. Virtually every member of the Fabian Society, from which emerged the Labor Party, was an ardent and vocal supporter, including Irish poet and playwright W. B. Yeats (1865–1939); the leader of the British suffragette movement Emmeline Pankhurst (1858–1928); Labor Prime

Minister Ramsay MacDonald (1866–1937); and economist and social reformer William Beveridge (1879–1963).

Irish playwright and cofounder of the London School of Economics George Bernard Shaw (1856–1950) was convinced that the future of socialism lay in what he called Social Darwinism and the "selective breeding of man." The philosopher Bertrand Russell (1872–1970) went one step further when he proposed that the state should issue everyone with color-coded "procreation tickets," and anyone caught having sexual relations with a partner of a differently colored card should be given a hefty fine or even face imprisonment for "genetic treason."

Meanwhile, in America eugenics had gathered significant momentum, which would go on to influence Hitler, the man who took it to a sickeningly "logical" conclusion. But the concept of a blond-haired, blue-eyed Nordic super-race did not originate with the Führer; he derived the idea from studying the Californian eugenics program that kicked off in 1909. It was the first state to enshrine eugenics principles in its legislation, and the Californian eugenics program allowed for the enforced isolation and sterilization of unfit individuals (with the definition of "unfit" left wide open to interpretation), and marriage restriction laws. Before the eugenics program was finally eradicated in America, more than 60,000 "unfit individuals" would be forcibly sterilized and as many marriages ruled illegal, with California alone accounting for roughly one third of that total.

MINI MYTH
IN EVERYBODY'S WELFARE

In 1942, William Beveridge gave a report that led to the rise of the British Welfare State. As a result, he is remembered as a kindly liberal. However, the social and health institutions Britain has today bear little resemblance to the selective ones that Beveridge had in mind. While he appreciated that the state should support those unable to find work, Beveridge believed those who received benefits should lose "all citizen rights—including not only the franchise but civil freedom and fatherhood."

Beveridge's plan was for the whole state support structure to be crafted in such a way as to encourage the breeding of the middle and upper classes, who would receive far more benefits than the lower classes, who would be repressed by their own strain. On the very night his report was being debated in Westminster, Beveridge addressed the Eugenics Society to assure the nervous members that this should indeed be the result. Mercifully this was not how the report eventually went through in 1945.

CALIFORNIA DREAMING

Without the financial muscle of the Carnegie Institution, the Rockefeller Foundation, and that of countless industrial magnates, the Eugenics Program of America would have undoubtedly floundered. It also received verbal backing from a majority of the Ivy League institutions, with Stanford's president David Starr Jordan's *The Blood of the Nation* published in 1902 in support of the eugenics movement. In 1904, the Carnegie Institution began funding the Eugenics Records Office (ERO) at a laboratory complex on Long

This still from the 1965 film Ordinary Fascism *shows a man's head being measured to test for Aryan qualities.*

Island. It was there that millions of index cards catalogued the lineage and identified patterns of inherited conditions of American citizens, which the ERO used to justify its often successful demands for the expansion of eugenics legislation and an intensification and broadening of the sterilization schemes. The computer technology company IBM would later copy these record-keeping methods when it developed a punch-card system to help Hitler run his own eugenics program. The infamous tattoo on concentration camp inmates' inner forearms was not just a numeric ID, it was their IBM number in which was coded race, deviancy, and skill—"Dutch, communist, carpenter," for example.

EUGENICIDE

American eugenics took a seriously dark turn with the publication in 1911 of the Carnegie-supported preliminary report by the American Breeders' Association on "The Best Practical Means for Cutting off the Defective Germ-Plasm in the Human Population." This presented an eighteen-point agendum in which point eight explored the use of euthanasia for the most hopeless of all cases. The commonly suggested form of "eugenicide" was by lethal gas chamber, a term and "solution" that would soon become all too distressingly familiar.

In 1918, Paul Popenoe (1888–1979), prominent eugenicist and US Army medical specialist in venereal diseases, coauthored *Applied Eugenics* with Roswell H. Johnson. The authors argued that, "From an historical point of view, the first method which presents itself is execution and its value in keeping up the standard of the race should not be underestimated." Popenoe was convinced that the infanticide employed in Ancient Rome and Sparta, as a birth-control method for unburdening the state of infants that showed signs of weakness or physical imperfection, was a model well worth exploring.

BUCK VS. BELL

The "science" of eugenics showed little sign of waning when in 1928 the Supreme Court chose to uphold a statute that promoted the compulsory sterilization of the unfit during the landmark case of Buck vs. Bell. The case centered on rape victim Carrie Buck (1906–83), who was impregnated by her attacker and then committed by her foster parents, John and Alice Dobbs, to the Virginia State Colony for Epileptics and the Feeble-Minded. With their own nephew the prime suspect, the Dobbs family raced to have Carrie committed as "incompetent and promiscuous," with the eugenics lobby hotly demanding she be sterilized after she gives birth. They alleged her natural mother had also been promiscuous and "sub-normal" and, although untrue, the court accepted the slur without question.

The case sat before Justice Oliver Wendell Holmes, the acclaimed physician, writer, and poet. He sanctioned the enforced sterilization, pronouncing, "It is better for all the world, if instead of waiting to execute degenerate offspring for crime, or to let them starve for their imbecility, society can prevent those who are manifestly unfit from continuing their kind. Three generations of imbeciles are enough."

This was both unfair and untrue: The child born as a result of the rape, Vivian, was a perfectly normal girl who did well at school but died, aged eight, of enteric colitis. Nevertheless, close tabs were kept on Carrie's other relatives, most probably by the ERO. Carrie's sister, Doris, was forced to undergo surgery that she was told was an appendectomy but was in fact a sterilization done in order to "terminate the family pollution of society." She did not find out the truth until she was 67.

Carrie lived into her seventies, a lifelong and avid reader, and those who found themselves partnered against her at bridge had no call to think her "feeble-minded." Justice Holmes's shameful summing up of the case was later quoted back to the American judges presiding over the Nazi Nuremberg war trials by the defendants' council.

A MATCH MADE IN HEAVEN

In 1934 the founder of the California State University at Sacramento and leading light of the Californian eugenics program, Charles M. Goethe (1875–1966), accepted an invitation from Germany to observe its developments in the area of eugenics. Although Germany's population was far smaller than that of the United States, its sterilizations by then were already exceeding 5,000 per month. Upon his return to California, Goethe gathered together his fellow eugenics committee members to congratulate them:

> You will be interested to know that your work has played a powerful part in shaping the opinions of the group of intellectuals who are behind Hitler in this epoch-making program. Everywhere I sensed that their opinions have been tremendously stimulated by American thought. I want you, my dear friends, to carry this thought with you for the rest of your lives, that you have really jolted into action a great government of 60 million people.

But the darkest link between the established American eugenics programs and Germany had in fact been forged earlier, when the Rockefeller Foundation had helped to establish the German eugenics program. The foundation had sent approximately $4 million (at today's value) in donations to several dubious German research projects; the Kaiser Wilhelm Institute for Anthropology, Human Heredity and Eugenics in Berlin was the major beneficiary.

For quite some time the American eugenics lobby had been thwarted in its dubious desires to conduct experiments on twins, but with Hitler they saw the chance to do so by proxy. On May 13, 1932, the foundation's New York

office cabled its Paris counterpart with the following mis-
sive: "JUNE MEETING EXECUTIVE COMMITTEE
NINE THOUSAND DOLLARS OVER THREE YEAR
PERIOD TO KWG INSTITUTE ANTHROPOLOGY
FOR RESEARCH ON TWINS AND EFFECTS ON
LATER GENERATIONS OF SUBSTANCES TOXIC
FOR GERM PLASM."

At the time, the Head of the Institute of Anthropology,
Human Heredity and Eugenics was Otmar Freiherr von
Verschuer (1896–1969), a man well known in American
eugenics circles, and whose gruesome assistants Josef
Mengele (1911–79) and Karin Magnussen (1908–1997)
would later achieve their own notoriety. But it was here,
under Verschuer and with Rockefeller money, that Mengele
started on the road that led him to the SS and Auschwitz,
and further unspeakable experiments on twins.

As World War II drew closer, the Rockefeller Foundation suspended all funding, but the Verschuer-Mengele program had by then assumed a life and will of its own. From
Auschwitz, Mengele would send off all manner of tissue
and blood samples from twins he had infected with diseases
ranging from typhus to syphilis. To Magnussen he sent
twins' eyes, especially those of any pair unlucky enough to
have eyes of a different color to each other, her particular
area of interest. Extraordinarily, and despite loads of evidence pointing to Verschuer and Magnussen's culpability,
they were both spared prosecution as war criminals.

In July 1946 when the war was over, Popenoe and Verschuer resumed their correspondence, with the former informing the latter, "It was indeed a pleasure to hear from you again. I have been very anxious about my colleagues in Germany. I suppose sterilization has been discontinued [there]?" Some people just don't know when to give up.

Within a matter of a few years, and like so many other American and German eugenicists, Verschuer had successfully re-branded himself as a geneticist. He assumed a comfortable professorship at the University of Münster, became a valued member of the American Society of Human Genetics, and yet all the while he maintained, until his death, that he had accepted his membership to the American Eugenics Society *during* the war.

MINI MYTHS
WELL, I NEVER!
POPULAR SCIENTIFIC IDEAS DEBUNKED

- When your arm goes to sleep it is not due to inhibited blood flow.
- Eyeballs cannot be removed from their sockets for treatment and then popped back in again.
- Sugar does not make kids hyperactive.

The Earth is flat.

The theory of a flat Earth immediately brings to mind those who had derided Christopher Columbus's ambition to sail around the world by claiming he would simply sail off the edge of the Earth. In reality, very few people in Columbus's time thought the Earth was flat; the notion that it had been an accepted idea was invented in the mid-nineteenth century by the humorist Washington Irving (1783–1859) in his hugely popular book *The Life and Voyages of Christopher Columbus* (1828). Irving concocted an entirely false account of Columbus's confrontation with the Salamancan Committee, complete with fabricated quotes attributed to idiotic clerics who allegedly spouted spurious notions of a flat Earth.

As events actually transpired, the Salamancan Committee objected to what they thought was Columbus's gross underestimation of the expanse of water he was proposing to cross. They were right and Columbus was wrong — the world was twice the size of the explorer's estimations. Nevertheless, the notion of a flat Earth was both ancient and pervasive, and it is also still adhered to by some. Perhaps the inspiration for Irving's prank was the fact that the medieval Church was chock-full of diehard flat-earthers.

Columbus—with globe—before the court

ELEPHANTS AND TURTLES

Hindu cosmology suggested the Earth was a flat-bottomed dome that was carried on the back of four elephants, which in turn stood on a giant turtle that swam in an infinite ocean. The Babylonians, too, were flat-earthers. They believed the globe was a disc floating in the sea, surrounded by a rim of mountains that supported the heavens. The ancient Egyptians also believed the earth to be flat, except their version saw the earth as rectangular shaped, with Egypt, naturally enough, situated in the center.

In much the same way, during the Middle Ages early European flat-earthers believed in a flat and square Earth because the Bible (Rev. 7:1) makes reference to the four corners of the Earth, each of which was guarded by angels who controlled the four winds. This was a time when the Church reserved the right to burn alive anyone who challenged the word of the good book.

The world according to Hindu cosmology

AGAINST THE ODDS

It is difficult, with hindsight, to see how such folly was allowed to triumph over proof to the contrary. The Ancient
Greeks had realized the Earth was a sphere simply by ob-
serving how inbound ships were first visible by the tip of their
masts, with the rest of the vessel rising into view as it drew
closer. They were extensive travelers and soon deduced that
as their location changed, so, too, did their relationship to
the stars, with some disappearing from view while new ones
appeared. They also observed that no matter how far they
sailed, the inclination all around them, from the horizons to
the skies, remained the same. This cone of inclination they
called the *klima*, hence "climb," and the changing weather
within any one such cone was the climate. Come the Middle
Ages, few with any intelligence thought the Greeks wrong,
but few with a love of life were prepared to defy the Church.

Pope Gregory the Great (540–604) openly proclaimed
it to be heresy to denounce the concept of a flat Earth, and
as late as the sixteenth century Pope Alexander VI (1431–
1503) was still maintaining the same stance. Better known
as Roderic Borja, Alexander VI had no difficulty reconcil-
ing his penchant for rape and murder with his Christian
ethics but, although a somewhat savvy and hand-to-throat
political survivor, Borja lacked intelligence.

He was also pretty greedy, and by 1493 he had wearied
of the two leading Catholic nations, Spain and Portugal,

fighting each other over new territories during the Age of Discovery—while the countries fought between themselves they were failing to fill Borja's Vatican coffers. As a dedicated flat-earther, Borja decided to draw a line down the map (the first to be called a Demarcation Line) and pronounced that the Portuguese hunt to the east of the line and the Spanish to the west. (The line cut through South America, which is why Portuguese is spoken in Brazil, and Spanish elsewhere.) But it never occurred to Borja that the Portuguese could simply keep sailing east to end up in the west.

MINI MYTH
JUDGMENT DAY

Flat-earthers were not all on the Catholic side of the fence. Although the German monk Martin Luther (1483–1546) today enjoys a reputation as a gentle, pious, and measured man, he was in fact a deeply unpleasant and small-minded anti-Semite who thought that all Jews should be covered in excrement and whipped out of town; he thought, too, that the poor and downtrodden should be treated no better because that is what God intended. Having an extremely small-minded perspective, Luther was also a flat-earther. His reasoning stemmed from the fact that all humanity was destined to witness the Second Coming on Judgment Day, and, if the earth were a sphere, the view of the majority of the planet's population would be obscured.

*This illustration of a globe, dated 1492,
rejects the theory of a flat earth.*

DETRACTORS IN THE MIDST

One of the few who dared to speak out against the flat-earth theory was Portuguese explorer Ferdinand Magellan (1480–1521), who, prior to embarking on his famous circumnavigation of 1519, pronounced, "The Church says the earth is flat but I have seen its shadow on the Moon and I have more faith in that shadow than I do in the Church." Having spoken so boldly, he had the presence of mind to board his ship and set sail. Eventually, as circumnavigations became more frequent, the Vatican was forced to admit that perhaps the earth was a sphere. Flat-earth thinking staggered on in a few fringe fundamentalist groups, mainly in America, but strange concepts of the form and profile of the Earth were not dead—even in the twentieth century.

JUMPING ON THE BANDWAGON

Far from being a rational man, Hitler, too, explored the flat-earth theory (as well as, quite conversely, the hollow-earth theory; see page 147) and finally decided that, although not flat, the earth was perhaps concave. He believed humanity ran around, upside down, on the interior of the surface, much like an army of ants. To explore this notion he ordered the German-born scientist Wernher von Braun (1912–77) to fire a series of rockets at a 45-degree angle in order to see if they landed in Australia. As the church of old had been before him, Hitler was by this point very much in charge, so von Braun nodded solemnly and set out on the doomed mission. Naturally hestitant to report his failure to hit Down Under, von Braun gently guided the Führer to the notion that, while the theory of a flat Earth may well be correct, the

An artistic representation of Columbus's arrival at Margarita Island in 1498

rockets did not contain the power necessary to validate it. Hitler seemed appeased, and von Braun made a sharp exit. But the Führer's fascination did not end there.

In April 1942, Hitler organized another attempt to prove himself right. Under the leadership of Dr. Heinz Fischer, a specialist in the field of infrared rays, an expedition was dispatched to Rügen Island in the Baltic Sea to attempt the same experiment, but this time with the aid of radar. For weeks on end the radar scanned at a 45-degree angle but nothing came back, leaving Fischer and his team extremely nervous about returning home. But they did not have to worry; by this time Hitler's attentions had been diverted to the invasion of Russia, which allowed the members of the expedition to slip quietly back into Germany unnoticed.

MINI MYTH
THE FINAL FRONTIER: SPACE GETS SILLY

Space was once home to the following nutty theories:

- Canals exist on Mars.
- The moon is a hollow vessel.
- The universe is static and does not expand.
- The hypothetical planet Vulcan orbits between Mercury and the sun.
- A full moon causes lunacy (see box on page 158).

Humans can be influenced by subliminal messaging.

Of all the discredited theories described in *They Got It Wrong: Science*, the one explored in this chapter is not only the most modern, it is also the most responsible for encouraging spin-offs of spurious science than any other notion.

MAD MEN

America during the late 1950s was a consumer's temple in which marketing men served as high priests. In 1957, market researcher James Vicary (1915–77) arrived on the scene, holding aloft the invisible Holy Grail of advertising.

Vicary reported the incredible successes he claimed he had achieved in conducting covert experiments in a public cinema in Fort Lee, New Jersey, in the summer of that same year. Vicary quite logically reasoned that consumers possessed a personal level of in-built sales resistance. He suggested that while their hearts may want the product, the ad-man's greatest enemy—the consumer's brain—was sitting in ultimate control, warning the owner. So, argued Vicary, why not cut the conscious brain out of the equation?

Vicary claimed that over a period of sixteen weeks he had exposed 45,000 cinema-goers to doctored versions of whichever film they had gone to watch. Using a tachisto-scope, an instrument used to display an image for a brief pe-riod, Vicary had incorporated flash-images that instructed audiences to "drink Coke" and "eat popcorn." Supporting his research with genuine science as to how fast the human eye can capture images and why, Vicary informed Madison

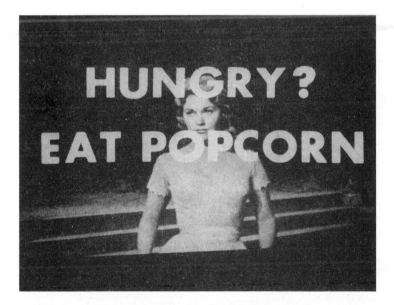

Hungry? Eat popcorn:
a mock-up of Vicary's experiment

Avenue ad gurus that his images endured for 1/3000 of a second—too fast for the eye and the conscious brain to notice, but detectable nonetheless on a subliminal level.

Because the brain had been influenced on an almost hypnotic level, no defensive actions had been activated. The result, claimed Vicary, had been an increase in the lobby sales of Coke and popcorn: They had risen by 18 percent and 57 percent, respectively. American manufacturers were agog; it all seemed to make perfect sense. The commercial worth of the carrot dangled before their collective eyes was deemed to be inestimable.

MINI MYTH
LIGHTS, CAMERA, ACTION: PHYSICS-GONE-WRONG IN THE MOVIES

- Victims of gunfire shots would never be flung backward because every action has an equal and opposite reaction.
- There is no such thing as a silencer that can reduce the noise of a gunshot to a muted *phut*.
- Quicksand does not cause drowning, because it's hundreds of times more buoyant than the Dead Sea.
- People ejected into space don't explode or experience boiling of the blood.

POLITICAL TWIST

Others, too, were excited by the possibilities offered by Vicary's discoveries, although their agendas hid an altogether more sinister edge. Political parties debated the possibility of using such tactics not only in their own television broadcasts but also during popular shows that were unrelated to politics.

There was a sudden and undignified scramble in the political arena as vast salaries were offered as incentives to entice opinion makers and so-called Depth Men (psychological manipulators) away from their Madison Avenue desks and up to Capitol Hill. Journalist Vance Packard published his still-famous *The Hidden Persuaders* (1957), which linked Washington's use of commercial advertising tactics to Vicary's experiment. Science fiction author Aldous Huxley told anyone who would listen that his *Brave New World* (1931) had come to hideous life, with Vicary "sounding the death knell of free will." And, as the debate over the ethicality of subliminal messaging rose to fever pitch, Richard Condon published *The Manchurian Candidate* (1959). A thriller that features the brainwashing of individuals by political parties, Condon's novel fanned the flames of conspiracy.

BRAINWASHING

Vicary could not have picked a better time for his fraud— for fraud is what it was—as America was still smarting from recent revelations that had emerged after the Korean War (1950–53). The sensationalist writer Edward Hunter's *Brain-washing in Red China* (1951)—which introduced the term "brainwashing" to the American people—induced paranoia among Americans by presenting images of shadowy Fu Manchu–like characters manipulating the minds of American POWs.

In reality, there had been no mind-bending experiments—apart from the CIA's notorious Project MK-Ultra (see below)—Hunter was simply weaving a web of lies. In truth, the Chinese did run re-educational programs for any prisoner who wanted to attend. Referred to as *szu-hsiang-kai-tsao*, or thought reform after mind cleansing, these programs were an attempt to rid the POWs' minds of their preconceived notions of Communist China and replace those "Western lies" with "the truth." There were no drugs, no hypnotists, no beatings; just boring lessons. That said, more than 2,000 POWs refused repatriation to America after the war, and America therefore needed to believe they had been induced to do so by indomitable means rather than by choice.

A SINISTER TURN

Perhaps unsurprisingly, the CIA, too, was more than a little interested in Vicary's experiments. In their postwar, clandestine Operation Paperclip (authorized by President Truman in 1945), the CIA had spirited back to America numerous Nazi scientists and doctors, some of whom had used death camp inmates in various psychotropic and sensory-deprivation experiments in their own attempts to achieve total mind control. More than thirty war criminals were given new identities and employed in the setup of the decidedly sinister MK-Ultra program, which used unwitting members of the public in a series of dangerous and, in some cases, lethal psychotropic experiments.

The program was petering out by 1957, but it seems that Vicary unwittingly breathed new life into it. A recently released CIA report dated January 17, 1958, conjectured:

It might be that in order to lessen the resistance of an individual to the hypnotic induction process, the use of subliminal projection may be considered. This technique has achieved success in commercial advertising, as "eat popcorn" or "drink Coke" projected in certain movie theaters for 1/3000-of-a-second intervals. It may be that subliminal projection can also be utilized in such a way as to feature a visual suggestion such as "Obey [deleted]," or "Obey [deleted]"—with similar success.

THE LID IS LIFTED

The 1952 production of an animated version of George Or-
well's *Animal Farm* had been a CIA-funded initiative and
flash-messaged re-screenings were organized, but the experiment failed to yield any results. And while the CIA remained in a state of confused frustration in their attempts to
manipulate whole cinema audiences into a certain frame of
mind, or to undertake certain actions immediately on leaving the auditoria, American and Canadian broadcasting
networks were equally unsuccessful in their own attempts
to replicate Vicary's results.

The most publicized of these independent experiments
was carried out by the Canadian Broadcasting Corporation
during its much-viewed Sunday night show *Close Up*. During the program, invitations to the viewers to phone in to
the station were flashed on the screen nearly 400 times, but
the station did not receive a single call.

The next nail in the subliminal-message coffin was
hammered home by Dr. Henry C. Link, director of the
Psychological Corporation. He invited Vicary to demon-
strate the supposedly incredible power of his technique
under controlled conditions, with Vicary failing on all
fronts.

Then, in 1958, Stuart Rogers, a student of psychology
at New York's Hofstra University, visited Fort Lee, the
home of Vicary's original experiment, to ask some very

direct questions that had not yet been asked. When Rogers spotted the small local cinema where Vicary had carried out his experiment he was immediately struck by its size—it was much too small to have accommodated the numbers claimed by Vicary over the indicated time span. After an interrogation from Rogers, the manager of the cinema admitted that no such experiments had taken place.

MINI MYTH
THE ANGELS OF MONS

As the case of James Vicary suggests, once a nation has taken an idea to heart, it becomes very difficult to persuade its members otherwise. Much the same happened to the British writer Arthur Machen, whose creations spawned the legend of the Angels of Mons. The entirely fictitious story described how a host of angels protected British soldiers on the World War I battlefields, holding back the crazed Huns with flaming swords and arrows. Although it was only a story, hordes of troops, officers, and chaplains, both Allied and German, claimed to have witnessed the event for themselves. Machen's reward for trying to remind the nation that it was but a whim of his own invention was a horsewhipping from an outraged bishop who collared him on Oxford Street.

CARRYING ON REGARDLESS

Finally, in 1962, Vicary himself admitted that it had been a scam: There was no such thing as subliminal messaging. He had invented it all in an attempt to save his failing consultancy. Despite these revelations, the bandwagon Vicary had so deftly put in motion refused to listen.

No matter how loud or how often Vicary protested that subliminal messaging was nothing more than a scam, the world failed to listen. Studies conducted in 2006 show that in America today, more than 80 percent of people—including those who work in advertising or teach psychology—still believe in the sinister power of subliminal messaging. Current opinion was certainly bolstered by the author Wilson Bryan Key (1925–2008), who during the 1970s and the 1980s became the self-styled guardian against such evils.

Despite impressive academic credentials, including a PhD in communications and a membership to Mensa, Key

MINI MYTH
666 OR 616?

Did you know that the original "number of the beast" is 616, not 666? Many new testament manuscripts refer to the number 666, but in older Greek texts it's 616. Movies, TV shows, and rock albums that have used 666 to symbolize evil may have been misled.

was a firm believer in the power of subliminal messaging. He claimed that three of the ice cubes in a Gilbey's Gin ad contained the letters S, E, and X discernible within their structure; he even saw the same word if the perforations along the edge of Ritz Crackers were joined together. Key stood watch for the Christian Right lobby, forcing the multinational product company Procter & Gamble to abandon its logo of a grey-bearded man posing as a moon because he claimed the figure "666," the number of the Beast (see box on facing page), was discernible in his facial hair.

ROCK 'N' ROLL SUICIDE

But still the corrupt legacy of James Vicary rolled on. Buoyed by the success of their farcical crusade against Procter & Gamble, the subliminal watchdogs turned their attention to Gothic-themed heavy rock groups. As far as Wilson Key was concerned, there had to be subliminal hooks somewhere in the equation to help explain the attraction of their blasphemous decadence. He reasoned that there must be a call to join the ranks of Satan in the words when played backward (backmasking). Naturally, everyone started playing their record collections backward, and the Christian Right believed this to have been the cause behind many teenage suicides, after the victims received "subliminal" orders to take their own lives.

So, according to Key and his like, not only was the brain

able to see images that normally escape the human eye, it could also listen to a record played normally, log the entire performance, and then play it in reverse in order to pick up any hidden subliminal message that may have been lurking in the lyrics. Quite a mental feat. Basically, no one wanted to accept the obvious: Teenagers who filled themselves up with drugs and were given to the darkness of goth-rock culture might simply be predisposed to self-harm. But matters came to a head with the suicide of American teenager Raymond Belknap and the attempted suicide of his friend James Vance on December 23, 1985.

Both young men had a history of drug abuse and depression and had allegedly spent the day smoking marijuana and listening to hours of music by the British heavy metal band Judas Priest. They then wandered off to a graveyard where Belknap blew his head off with a shotgun, leaving Vance to try the same; he survived but with horrific injuries. Wilson Key was trotted out as a professional witness on the power of subliminal messaging for a trial in which the rock group was charged with the notion that their track "Better By You, Better Than Me" carried embedded subliminal messages that had urged the boys to take their tragic actions.

Fortunately, the judge was not that gullible, and with Key's pronouncements discounted, the case was dismissed. As Judas Priest's lead singer, Rob Halford, would wryly observe after the case, "If I'd thought that sort of crap worked, we would have embedded messages telling everyone to go out and buy more of our records."

SPURIOUS SPIN-OFFS

The gullibility of the public at large is indeed an awesome market force. One might assume that if premise B is built on premise A, which is later proved to be a complete lie, then premise B would automatically go into the garbage can of history, along with its progenitor. Not so. Despite Vicary's very public admission that subliminal messaging had been a lie, spurious spin-offs had already been set well in motion.

Although the idea of sleep-learning had been quashed in 1956 with the electroencephalography studies conducted by Charles Simon and William H. Emmons of the Rand Corporation, Vicary's lie breathed new life into the notion. Commercial ventures sprang up across America and Europe, trumpeting the false promise of allowing us to tap into the fearsome powers hidden in the subconscious—if subliminal influence could exert such power when the subject was awake, its power would be even greater if the subject was asleep. It is just a pity there is no truth in the idea.

A multibillion-dollar industry has been built on the idea of sleep-learning, which—despite having been roundly debunked by prominent sleep experts and psychologists—

still refuses to go away. In studies conducted in 1991 participants were told that personal enhancement messages would be played to them while they slept to help make them more assertive. On waking, many participants did indeed proclaim themselves to feel more in control and behaved accordingly—despite having been subjected to messages telling them to be more humble and self-deprecating. In all such experiments, conducted under clinical conditions with the subjects wired up to an EEG to ensure they really were asleep, the knowledge impartation has been nil.

THE MOZART EFFECT

From subliminal messaging and sleep-learning stemmed the "Mozart Effect," a term coined in 1991 by the French ear, nose, and throat (ENT) specialist Dr. Alfred A. Tomatis (1920–2001). Tomatis claimed that listening to certain types of music was beneficial to certain conditions and conducive to the achievement of certain objectives, and he recommended Mozart to aid depression and concentrate the mind of those with learning difficulties to the task at hand.

Tomatis's international standing was so great that two University of California heavyweights, Dr. Frances Rauscher and Dr. Gordon Shaw, looked into the alleged phenomenon and published their results in the scientific journal *Nature*. For reasons only they could conjecture—perhaps concentrating on the music helped the mind to warm up—subjects who listened to Mozart before certain tests did indeed do better than those who had been left in silence.

The good doctors said they detected a slight and very transient improvement in participant's spatial-temporal reasoning powers and that "there appear to be pre-existing sites in the brain that respond to specific frequencies." They made no mention of individual participants' IQs, nor that other experiments had reported similar findings using the music of Meatloaf and Iron Maiden. Predictably the press reported that listening to Mozart makes your children smarter—the so-called Mozart effect was ripe for exploitation.

Despite Shaw and Rauscher protesting that their work had been completely misrepresented—that there was no correlation between the playing of Mozart and the listener's intelligence—the idea had been set in motion. In 1998 the governors of both Georgia and Tennessee announced programs to provide every newborn baby with music CDs, and new research was conducted into the awareness of the unborn child. Millions of mothers-to-be snapped up devices comprised of a CD player and an implement that resembled a reverse-stethoscope to bombard their unborn with Mozart, along with recordings of their own voices making positive affirmations of life. However, Georgia and Tennessee failed to become the cradles of *wunderkind*, and we have yet to read of the first child to launch into a rendition of *Don Giovanni* as the doctor slaps it into life.

MINI MYTHS
WELL, I NEVER!
POPULAR SCIENTIFIC IDEAS DEBUNKED

- We use all of our brains (well, at least some of us do!) and not just the 10 percent of myth.
- There is no harm in waking up a sleepwalker; in fact, it is best to do so.
- Leprosy cannot be transmitted by casual contact.
- 20/20 vision does not denote perfect eyesight, only that both eyes function normally at a twenty-foot range.

Cocaine and heroin can cure a range of man's ills.

Long before they were recognized as Class-A drugs, capable of destroying the lives of those who grow, import, and consume them, cocaine and opium were hailed as panaceas by the nineteenth-century medical profession. Eulogized as cures for a range of ills, the drugs were made readily available in numerous over-the-counter products, many of which were sponsored by leading doctors and prominent figures.

THE TREND CATCHES ON

Pope Leo XIII (1810–1903) never ventured far without a hip flask of the cocaine-laced French wine Vin Mariani; he even bestowed the Vatican Gold Medal on the manufacturers and allowed his image to be used in the promotion of the product, which was marketed to ailing children, pregnant women suffering from morning sickness, or those feeling just a little under the weather. At that time, everyone

Cocaine-infused Vin Mariani:
the Pope's favorite

thought opium and cocaine to be of great benefit to mankind at large.

Mothers were also encouraged to use either drug to treat teething babies. Since the sixteenth century, misguided physicians had believed in the efficacy of slitting the gums of infants to help ease the emergence of the first teeth. The practice had gone into decline by the end of the eighteenth century, mainly for the distress it caused, but a century on it enjoyed a comeback as the pain of the incision could be followed with a direct application of one of these new "miracle anesthetics," after which no doubt the child just sat there chuckling.

With the medical profession trumpeting their merits, not to mention profiting from their mass production and sale, cocaine- and opium-based products were readily available; even grocers and clothing stores kept stocks for anyone caught short. And the hallmark of cynical advertising was all pervasive. All such drugs were recommended by an avuncular-looking medical consultant, sold under innocuous-sounding names such as Mrs. Winslow's Soothing Syrup or Professor MacGuire's Infant's Panacea. The entire medical profession was united in the opinion that opiates and cocaine were valuable cures that contained no addictive qualities. But the medical professionals paid to investigate the nature of the two drugs were in fact voracious consumers themselves, so it was little wonder that their findings completely exonerated the drugs of any charges regarding their capacity to addict.

Soothing syrup for children: Mrs. Winslow gives her seal of approval

MINI MYTH
IF FREUD SAID IT'S OK . . .

The Austrian neurologist Sigmund Freud (1856–1939) championed cocaine not only as the ideal cure for opium and alcohol addiction but also as an appetite stimulant for those with anorexia and as a first-line treatment for asthma sufferers.

In *Über Coca* (1884) Freud applauded the drug's efficacy in stimulating "exhilaration and lasting euphoria, which in no way differs from the normal euphoria of the healthy person." Warming to his theme, Freud continued:

> You perceive an increase of self-control and possess more vitality and capacity for work. In other words, you are simply normal, and it is soon hard to believe you are under the influence of any drug.
>
> Long intensive physical work is performed without any fatigue. This result is enjoyed without any of the unpleasant after-effects that follow exhilaration brought about by alcohol. Absolutely no craving for the further use of cocaine appears after the first, or even after repeated taking of the drug.

BEST OF BRITISH

Queen Victoria, on her physicians' advice, guzzled laudanum, a whole-opium tincture; she took cannabis for her menstrual pains; and, like her prime minister, William Gladstone, she also liked the occasional snort of cocaine. It is probably no exaggeration to say that, throughout the greater part of the nineteenth century, the British ruling class and half of the population lived in a drug fog. And why not? The government in Victoria's day was the most aggressive drug cartel the world has yet seen. They even made the Colombian warlords look like amateurs. The UK's domestic imports of raw opium in 1830 had been alarming enough—just short of 100,000 one-pound blocks; by 1860 this had rocketed to just under 300,000 pounds.

It was the British who so dramatically expanded the poppy fields of Northern India and Afghanistan, the deadly results of which still reverberate today. Desperate to find new markets, the British Empire targeted China, despite the country's already serious opiate problem, with a total of approximately 2 million addicts. Regardless, taking advantage of the opportunity, the British began shipping great quantities of the drug to expand that user base. When the Chinese objected and demanded the trade cease, the good Victorians attacked Canton, the means by which China controlled trade with the West, in the First Opium War (1839–42).

The British emerged victorious and demanded from

China a host of concessions in the Treaty of Nanking, which included ceding Hong Kong to Queen Victoria. The Chinese were reluctant to adhere to all of the treaty's terms, leading the British to initiate another attack in the Second Opium War (1856–60). The British again emerged victorious. They added Kowloon to their previous acquisition, forced the Chinese to legalize an opium trade that was destroying their people, and began the wholesale transportation of "indentured Chinese laborers" (slaves, in other words) to the Americas to toil on the railways. China had no choice, and within a matter of years the British government had acquired over 100 million opium customers in China alone.

MINI MYTH
MEDICINE MEN:
WHEN DOCTORS GOT IT WRONG

The following list of dubious medical procedures suggests the men of medicine haven't always got it right.

- Trepanation (drilling a hole in the skull) to cure all manner of ills.
- Lobotomies to "calm" the mentally ill.
- An insulin-induced coma to relieve the symptoms of schizophrenia.
- Hysterectomies to cure paranoia in women.

HOUSTON, WE HAVE A PROBLEM

The situation in America was no better. A staggering 10 million opium pills and more than 3 million ounces of other opiate preparations were dished out to the Union Army alone during the Civil War (1861–65). While the drugs may have helped the troops to get through the horrors of war, when the conflict was over and nearly 500,000 opium-habituated troops returned to civilian life, the medical profession was forced to acknowledge that the unrestricted use of such drugs might be somewhat of a problem.

Those who could afford to fund their habit could buy the drugs locally over the counter or through mail-order from medical suppliers who still upheld the common belief that these were harmless substances, even if put to recreational use. It was the antics of those who could *not* afford their habit that first gave cause for concern.

Backed by the American Medical Association, the Society for the Suppression of the Opium Trade renewed its attack on doctors who considered opiates and cocaine to be not only harmless but also broadly beneficial. In 1893, a Royal Commission on Opium was reluctantly convened to investigate. But this was a venture doomed from the start. Although the commission went through the correct channels, listened attentively to countless witnesses, and produced a suitably weighty report, it concluded that the use of opium was not responsible for a decline in moral standards or physical damage to the user. In fact, it decreed that opium in recreational use was no worse than alcohol, and that it had positive medical benefits.

The preeminent British medical journal *The Lancet* welcomed the findings, commenting that they "dealt a crushing blow to the anti-opium faddists whose claims were either ridiculously exaggerated or wholly unfounded." The problem with the commission was that it was a *Royal* Commission and, as such, directly answerable to the junkie-in-chief herself—and no one involved relished the prospect of confronting Queen Victoria with the realities of her own laudanum and cocaine usage.

MINI MYTH
DENS OF INIQUITY

Novels promoted the myth of opium dens run by Chinese immigrants, who supposedly teemed in London's Limehouse district. While the Chinese certainly ran opium parlors in American cities where they had been transported following the Second Opium War, the Chinese population was never more than a few hundred in nineteenth-century London. There is in fact no evidence of any such dens. Why go to a seedy den in a dangerous part of London when you could buy your stash in Mayfair?

STRAIGHT TO USER

Literature began to explore the sleazy and debilitating side of opium, with Conan Doyle's Dr. Watson expressing serious disapproval of Sherlock Holmes's use of a substance detrimental to his superior intellectual powers.

But few wanted to listen to the dissenting voices on the ill effects of opiates and cocaine, and the medical profession

An artistic representation of one of London's fabled opium dens

vehemently defended its stance. In 1885 the American pharmaceutical company Parke-Davis augmented its cocaine product range with a solution that could be injected directly into the user's veins. It was sold in a variety of main-street shops, complete with syringe and backed by an advertising campaign that claimed it would "supplant the need for food, make cowards brave, make the timid loquacious and render the user insensitive to pain."

SERVING THE MASS MARKET

In 1898 the German pharmaceutical company Bayer synthesized a new and highly addictive opioid, which they marketed as an over-the-counter product under the brand name of Heroin, for the supposed heroic feelings it engendered in

Over-the-counter: one of German pharmaceutical company Bayer's heroin products

the user. Again, the medical profession welcomed this advance without question and advocated the use of heroin for the treatment of colds and flu, bronchitis, whooping cough, and for pregnant women suffering from morning sickness.

Developments continued in America, where Confederate veteran doctor John Stith Pemberton (1831–88) invented a new cocaine-laced wine to rival Pope Leo XIII's favorite, Vin Mariani. First marketed as Pemberton's Brain Tonic, this lethal mix of alcohol and cocaine proved very popular, until 1886 when Pemberton's hometown of Atlanta, Georgia, objected to its alcohol content, forcing the doctor to create a Temperance-friendly version. It was this blend of cocaine-laced syrup and soda water that evolved into Coca-Cola. But the manufacturer became increasingly uneasy about the drug element in response to the growing notion in the South that cocaine usage was driving black men to rape white women. In 1903 all traces of cocaine had been stripped from the drink.

NEW GAME IN TOWN

By then the writing was on the wall for the continued free availability of cocaine and heroin. It had dawned on the majority of the medical profession that the unchecked use of these drugs was not the answer to the people's minor ailments. That said, the possession and use of cocaine remained unlegislated in America until 1970.

More than just a thirst quencher:
Coca Cola was advertised as a
stimulant to help relieve exhaustion.

Meanwhile, by the 1950s the Americans had taken to heart another "harmless" drug—amphetamine. Doctors on both sides of the Atlantic scattered these pills like confetti. Apparently they found them very useful to perk up patients in hospital, and everyone was buying Benzedrine inhalers over the counter. Throughout the 1950s, Pan-Am's in-flight courtesy packs for passengers included a Benzedrine inhaler, which the accompanying pamphlet advised "would make the flight more pleasant and seem to pass more quickly." No kidding!

Disease is caused by foul smell and lack of personal hygiene.

Known by many as the father of germ theory, the French chemist and microbiologist Louis Pasteur (1822–95) conducted a series of experiments in the second half of the nineteenth century that conclusively proved germs cause disease. Before Pasteur's discoveries, the overwhelming majority of the medical and scientific communities, including pioneering nurse Florence Nightingale (1820–1910), had publicly ridiculed the idea that organisms undetectable to the human eye could invade the body, breed in sufficient numbers, and bring about the death of the host.

MAKING A STINK

Until Pasteur's irrefutable evidence was published, the "miasma theory" held sway. This concept maintained that all disease was caused by foul smells, lack of personal hygiene, and, to a lesser extent, impurity of the mind and soul. Florence Nightingale certainly adhered to this notion. Her complicity may have caused thousands of deaths in the Crimea, where she thought that clean surroundings and regular Bible readings would put a patient on the road to recovery.

Back in the sixteenth century the infection theory was once advanced. The Italian physician Girolamo Fracastoro (1478–1553) believed that infective agents called spores were responsible for the spread of germs and viruses; he warned that these spores could transfer infection by direct or indirect means. He also wrote that "such things as clothes, linen, etc., which although not themselves corrupt, can nevertheless foster the essential seeds of the contagion and thus cause infection." Although Fracastoro was on the right track, it was to be approximately another 300 years before the Italian physician Agostino Bassi (1773–1856) made the first identification of living organisms as the cause of disease.

GERMINATION

In 1835, Italian silk production was in danger of collapse because the silkworms had fallen prey to an invasion of parasitic mites. Bassi made note of the white, powdery coating of spores found on the dead and dying silkworms, and he became the first to make the correct connection between infective invasion and disease. Thirty years later, when the French silk industry fell prey to the same parasite, Louis Pasteur, inspired by the work of Bassi, came to the same conclusion, although, in Pasteur's defense, he had

MINI MYTH
BY THE POWER OF GOD . . .

Before the miasma theory gained ground, the majority of the Ancient civilizations believed disease to be a punishment inflicted by the gods. Although detractors did exist: *Atharvaveda*, the sacred Hindu text written toward the end of the second millennium BCE, suggested living causative agents were responsible for disease; although the text did not elaborate on the size and nature of the agents, so it may have been nothing more than guesswork.

Marcus Terentius Varro (116–27 BCE), a Roman physician and polymath, was the next to suggest something more than bad air and foul smells might be responsible for disease. Not only did he caution people against building homes near swamps, he even suggested they refrain from frequenting them, because proliferating therein were "certain minute creatures that cannot be seen by the eyes, which float in the air and enter the body through the mouth and nose and there cause serious diseases." But few paid attention to Marcus Terentius; majority opinion held the gods to be responsible.

by that point already made major inroads into the discovery of germ theory.

As Bassi had before him, Pasteur recommended the separation of the colonies of silkworms into disinfected farms and the immediate destruction of any silkworm that showed

This front page of a French newspaper from 1912
depicts Death carrying cholera.

signs of infection. Despite these quarantines and precautions having twice eradicated the epidemic, the medical and scientific communities were not prepared to listen. The majority of opinion still held that all disease—cholera, typhoid, malaria, to name only a few—was the inevitable progeny of foul smells. In Austria, Pasteur's contemporary Ignaz Semmelweis (1818–65) was also leading a case against miasma theory, but so vehement were his attacks that it would eventually lead to his murder by a group of some of the most prominent medical figures in Austrian medicine.

PLEASE WASH YOUR HANDS

Death rates of approximately 20 percent for mothers and offspring during childbirth were considered quite normal in some clinics in the mid-nineteenth century. This included the First Obstetrical Clinic in a Viennese hospital, which offered benefits to expectant mothers if they volunteered themselves as guinea pigs for new doctors.

There were two maternity clinics at the hospital. Semmelweis took up his position as senior resident at the First Obstetrical Clinic in 1846 but was puzzled to find that the childbirth death rate at the Second Clinic was a mere 2 percent — 18 percent lower than the First Clinic. The only difference between the two institutions was that no autopsies were conducted at the Second Clinic. His second clue came from the patients themselves. Having noticed that something was seriously awry at the First Clinic, a good number of Vienna's pregnant women contrived to give birth en route to the First Clinic so they could still get the benefits promised by the program without having to run the gauntlet of its professional care.

Semmelweis was staggered to find that the death rate in this forward-thinking group was almost nonexistent.

Semmelweis's predictions were confirmed with the sudden death of his good friend, professor of forensics Jakob Kolletschka, in 1847. Kolletschka had been supervising a student conducting an autopsy on a patient who had died of puerperal (childbirth) fever in the First Clinic, and within three days of being nicked by a carelessly brandished scalpel, he was himself dead of the same condition.

Focusing his attentions on the autopsy rooms, the first thing Semmelweis noted was that students and professors

Ignaz Semmelweis with mother and child

routinely left them without washing and headed straight to the treatment and examination rooms. He immediately instituted a regime of hand washing in a solution of chlorinated lime, and the death rate fell by 90 percent overnight. Within two months it was nil. However, instead of being hailed a hero, Semmelweis was harassed out of his post by colleagues offended at being ordered to wash their hands like naughty schoolboys. What possible correlation could there have been between the hand-washing fiasco and the fall in the death rate?

MINI MYTHS
WELL, I NEVER!
POPULAR SCIENTIFIC IDEAS DEBUNKED

- Edison did not invent the lightbulb.
- Benjamin Franklin did not invent the so-called Franklin stove.
- Pythagoras did not come up with "his" eponymous theorem.
- The Wright brothers were not the first to achieve powered flight.
- Alexander Bell was not responsible for inventing the telephone.

THE COLD SHOULDER

When Semmelweis left the clinic, the death rate returned to its original position. In every subsequent post he took up, Semmelweis instituted the same hand-washing regime and the death rate plummeted, but his old enemies had him pushed out of every subsequent position he assumed—and the death rate rose in his wake. And *still* nobody listened. Unbelievably, the Viennese Medical Council saw Semmelweis as a troublemaker who was intent on blaming patient and infant death on some of its more influential members. The same members who felt it was their right to poke around inside patients with hands still dripping with germs.

Lit hygiénique.   Lit antihygiénique.

*From an early twentieth century book on
the new rules of hygiene. The bed on the right was
thought to trap germs.*

Ridiculed as a fractious oddball, Semmelweis was cut out of the medical fraternity and marginalized. But he remained unrepentant. Continuing his campaign in exile, Semmelweis published an open letter to the obstetrics fraternity at large, which was, unfortunately for its sender, a little on the antagonistic side. Feeling that decisive action was needed, Semmelweis's enemies decided to have him declared insane and locked away where he could create no more waves.

In 1865, a small group of physicians led by Vienna's leading dermatologist, Ferdinand Ritter von Hebra (1816–80), lured Semmelweis to an asylum under the pretense that his opinion was sought on certain matters. As soon as Semmelweis was through the door he became suspicious and tried to leave, but von Hebra's henchmen were prepared and beat Semmelweis so badly that he died shortly after in one of the asylum's dungeons.

It is understandable that such entrenched and established opinion would be a large ship to turn, but when undisputable proof was clear for all to observe, it seems bizarre in the extreme that the only action the captains of that ship could think to take was to murder the messenger. But Semmelweis is not forgotten. In scientific circles, the "Semmelweis reflex" is a common expression used to describe the knee-jerk reaction of entrenched thinking to any suggestion that it might be wrong.

There is a missing link in the evolutionary chain.

T he notion that there is a missing link in the evolutionary chain, an early human ancestor who would help explain the full transition from ape to man, was an accepted idea of both paleontology and anthropology until the early part of the twentieth century.

The descent of man: a smooth transition that bore little relation to reality

THE SEARCH BEGINS

Although the concept has no basis in scientific fact, the search for the missing link among the archaeological community has persisted since the late nineteenth century. While many have sought proof of such a link, others believed they had found it. A contingent of nineteenth-century anthropologists believed it still stalked the more remote regions of the planet — one demented soul even tried to breed it, with consequences that still ravage the Third World to this day.

The Dutch paleontologist Eugène Dubois (1858–1940) was the first to embark on a planned search for evidence of a missing link. In 1890 he was digging up half of Java, Indonesia, in his quest. In the latter part of that year he dug a pit near the Solo River in Eastern Java and unearthed the remains of what would become known as "Java Man," an admittedly simian-like creature that Dubois immediately pronounced to *be* the missing link. Few believed him, and he drew so much ire from academics that he gathered up the bones and became a virtual recluse. Dubois finally allowed full examination of Java Man in 1923, when it was quickly established that his find was nothing more than an example of *Homo erectus* (upright man). Dubois retreated into obscurity, never again to communicate with academia.

Not content with discovering mere remains of the so-called missing link, other individuals have supported the notion that the missing link has not died out but is still with us. We speak, of course, of Bigfoot—also known as Sasquatch, the yeti, or the abominable snowman.

Since the mid- to late nineteenth century the popular press has peddled the notion of Bigfoot as a living missing link. A rather surprising coterie of academic heavyweights have stood firmly in this corner, including Grover Krantz (1931–2002), professor of anthropology at Washington State University, and his colleague Geoffrey Bourne (1909–88), director of the internationally respected Yerkes National Primate Research Center in Atlanta, Georgia.

Such a notion was supported by John Napier (1917–87), an anthropologist, a primatologist, and a leading light at the Smithsonian Institute. The celebrity anthropologist Margaret Mead (1901–78) also believed that hairy missing

The remains of "Java Man"

links still stalked the snowlines—however, she also believed guardian aliens were sent here to observe us and ensure civilization was kept on the straight and narrow.

In 1953, the explorer Sir Edmund Hillary reported seeing yeti tracks and mounted an expedition in 1960 to gather evidence of the beast's existence. In 1959, actor James Stewart took possession of a supposed skeletonized yeti hand that had been stolen from Tibetan monks. Stewart smuggled it out of India to London for examination, where primatologist William Charles Osmond established that the hand was in fact Neanderthal. The anthropologist Jeffrey Meldrum (1958–), a professor at Idaho State University, actually went in search of Bigfoot in Siberia in 2011, though his expedition failed to yield any results.

REALITY CHECK
IT FELT LIKE A GOOD IDEA AT THE TIME

In the 1950s the World Health Organization (WHO) decided to combat Borneo's malaria problem by killing mosquitoes with DDT spray. Although a success, the spraying also killed off the wasps that fed on the roof-munching thatch-caterpillar, which promptly de-roofed the homes in the local area. Lots of cats also died after trying to lick themselves clean, which meant the rat-population exploded. The RAF then parachuted in more than 10,000 hungry felines to deal with the problem!

Different skeletons in profile
(from left to right): gibbon, orangutan,
chimpanzee, gorilla, and man

JUST ONE PROBLEM

The problem is these investigations had no basis in scientific fact: No one, Darwin included, has ever suggested that man is descended from apes. Had it been the case then there would be no apes left—they too would have evolved and would doubtless now be running banks or taking up seats in Congress. And despite nineteenth-century academia presenting the concept of man's descent in linear form, with clearly defined stages of development and advancement, this is now known to be very widely off the mark.

Desmond Morris's book *The Naked Ape* (1967), which sought to compare humans to other animals, is partially responsible for suggesting man descends from apes, as are the ever-popular posters that depict the evolution of man as a series of figures that become increasingly upright and devoid of body hair. What Darwin and others had proposed was that man and primate shared a common progenitor before dividing to descend in parallel, rather than in sequence.

The traditional perception of the descent of man as a sequential series of neat changes is completely inaccurate. The slow development followed a multi-branched and rather untidy path, with some branches dying out and others coexisting and even interbreeding across millennia. There were no cleanly divided stages.

REALITY CHECK
THE DESCENT OF DOG

Many species, including cats and dogs, were once the same species with common roots in the prehistoric genus *Miacis*, an arboreal dog-like creature with retractable claws used for climbing. This ancient progenitor lived around 50 million years ago, and since then it has subdivided by dictate of its diverse environments to produce cats, dogs, weasels, bears, and hyenas. Yet no sensible person would propose that dogs were descended from cats. It is also worth mentioning here that the hyena is the very confused marker of the cat–dog divide because, for all its appearance and countless references to it as a pack-hunting dog, the hyena is in fact more closely related to cats, evolutionarily speaking.

LENGTHY DIVERGENCE

In 2006, the exploration of the complex history of the human genome conducted by David Reich, a population geneticist at Harvard, revealed that the divergence of proto-humans and proto-chimpanzees from their common progenitor was a more lengthy and complicated process than previously thought. Just as late Neanderthals and early modern man cohabited and interbred (see box on facing page), so, too, did proto-humans and proto-chimpanzees over several million years. The recent tracking of the X chromosome in both modern man and chimpanzees reveals that the final divergence of the two species did not actually occur until between 5 and 6 million years ago, approximately 1 million years later than previously thought. But this still does not give support to the spurious theory of a missing link; it just means that early humans and chimpanzees remained similar enough in appearance to find one another acceptable breeding partners for longer than was previously assumed after they divided from the common progenitor.

THE IDEA WILL NOT DIE

Despite the fact there has never existed a tidy chain in our evolution from which a link could go missing, the idea itself will not get lost. Creationists, driven into a frenzy of denial by the publication of Darwin's *On the Origin of the Species*

MINI MYTH
NOT SO NEANDERTHAL

After the remains of a Neanderthal man were found in 1856 in the Neander Valley, just to the east of Düsseldorf, academics rushed to brand him a brutal, hunched, and hairy club-wielding humanoid. In reality, the Neanderthal was a far more civilized being.

Although slightly shorter and stockier than his modern counterpart, Neanderthal man was no troglodytic dolt. Possessing a brain approximately 3.4 ounces (100 milliliters) *larger* than his modern counterpart, Neanderthal man built individual and group dwellings and kept himself warm with fires. He cooked meat and vegetables, had his own language, and produced tools as sophisticated as those of co-evolving modern man, with whom Neanderthal man socially interacted and crossbred, as the present gene pool proves. (Approximately 4 percent of the DNA in Europeans and Asians is Neanderthal.)

As for the once held belief that "primitive" Neanderthals were driven to their rightful extinction by the rise of so-called modern man, this too has been quashed. Advances in DNA indicate that Neanderthal man was simply absorbed into early Cro-Magnon stock and modified through interbreeding. Neanderthal man, therefore, did not die out—he is still with us, a fact that will come as no surprise to female readers.

(1859), denounced him for allegedly suggesting that man was evolved from apes rather than created by God. As previously stated (see page 63), Darwin never suggested anything of the kind, but the press, among others, decided this was the thrust of his work, and those who had never read Darwin's seminal book were so keen to attack that they leapt on this ready-to-ride bandwagon.

By the advent of the 1900s, a British amateur archaeologist named Charles Dawson (1864–1916) was making a name for himself after he dug up half of Sussex to unearth some pretty interesting finds. In 1912, Dawson dramatically announced a staggering discovery: He had found the missing link—the skeletal remains of the long-sought apeman—near the village of Piltdown, East Sussex.

It would be more than forty years before the "discovery" would be denounced as a fraud and the bones revealed to be the composite of a medieval human skull, the lower jaw of an orangutan, and chimpanzee teeth, all filed down to resemble a more human profile and appropriately aged in chemical solutions. But whether Dawson himself was the fraudster or had been unwittingly duped by another who had placed the find in his path has never been satisfactorily answered. It is, however, interesting to note that a near neighbor was Sir Arthur Conan Doyle, a man who was himself under heavy fire from the Christian Fundamentalists for his championing of the spiritualist movement. Not only was Doyle a resident of Piltdown, he was also, like

A.

B.

C.

Compare and contrast:
(a) the Piltdown skull, (b) a Neanderthal skull,
and (c) a modern human skull

An artistic reconstruction of the Piltdown man

Dawson, a member of the Sussex Archaeological Society. The two would often be seen huddled together deep in conversation in the run-up to the "discovery."

In 1953, *Time* magazine published an article that completely debunked the so-called Piltdown Man, but by then the damage had been done—the idea of the missing link had etched itself irretrievably on to the public's consciousness.

In 1974, skeleton bones found in Ethiopia heralded a

further renaissance in the missing link theory. Known as "Lucy" (so named because the Beatles' "Lucy in the Sky in Diamonds" was playing on the geologists' tape deck as the first bones were unearthed), the skeleton did indeed present the image of a three-million-year-old chimpanzee-like creature that bore indications in the pelvic structure and knee joints of having walked upright. The discovery of an older and taller male version of Lucy in Ethiopia in 2010 lead to further excitement within some circles about the prospect of a missing link. But no one involved in either dig had at any point suggested the finds were anything of the sort.

STAGED INTERVENTION

Now on to the man who decided to produce his own missing link—Stalin's own Dr. Frankenstein, Soviet biologist Ilya Ivanovich Ivanov (1870–1932) and his Humanzee Project of the late 1920s. As early as 1910, Ivanov was openly musing the feasibility of creating a living, breathing missing link by crossbreeding humans with chimpanzees, orangutans, and even gorillas. Few doubted him; this, after all, was the man who had already produced a zeedonk (a zebra crossed with a donkey) and crossbred or cross-inseminated a range of animals from cows with antelopes to rabbits with rats.

By 1925 Ivanov had secured Humanzee funding from

the Kremlin and, rightly thinking such experiments to be better conducted as far away from Moscow as possible, he and his son, also called Ilya, headed for the less stringently controlled environs of Africa. On a more sinister note, Ivanov considered Africa best suited for his program because, as "everybody knew," Africans are closer to our simian forebears than are white Europeans, and he was going to need human participants in his grotesque fiasco.

The summer of 1926 saw the Ivanovs ensconced in the city of Conakry, in what was then French New Guinea. But exactly what happened next is unclear. It is known that the first round of experiments centered on inseminating female chimpanzees with human sperm. However the methodology involved has been the subject of lurid speculation. Ivanov always refused to discuss his methods beyond stating that the donors had all been African men who had been "well paid for their input"—an unfortunate term given the nature of all contemporary and subsequent speculation.

The second round of experiments centered on African women inseminated with sperm donations from chimpanzees. But, again, just how many times this was tried and failed is unclear. By 1927 the French were disturbed by the unsettling rumors that had begun to circulate, and they obliged the Ivanovs to return to Russia, where they were given facilities in Sukhumi in Stalin's native Georgia. However, none of their experiments bore any results, and, in the time-honored tradition of Stalin's regime, the elder Ivanov was rewarded with a one-way ticket to exile, where he died a couple of years later.

REALITY CHECK
HALF-MAN–HALF-APE ARMY

Although there is no evidence that Ivanov knew of the Kremlin's motive for funding his bizarre set of experiments, it has since come to light that Stalin and Lavrentiy Beria, his secret-police chief, were keen to see if it would be possible to breed a whole new half-man–half-ape army. When not laboring uncomplainingly to harvest the country's resources in the inhospitable north, they would make ideal soldiers because chimps are instinctively tribal and much given to organized war in their natural environment. This, coupled with their ability to outrun Olympic sprinters and single-handedly pull up to 1,000 pounds on a torque bar, would have made Humanzees a fearsomely brutish and perhaps mindlessly obedient force. At least, that was what Stalin and Beria had hoped for.

DEVASTATING CONSEQUENCES

But the fallout from his folly may still be with us. Although HIV and AIDS was, until recently, thought by most to be a disease of the 1980s, it is now clear that SIV, the simian equivalent, somehow jumped the species barrier to become HIV some time in the late 1920s, with Guinea being a leading location for instances of infection.

When HIV was first identified as a variant of SIV, rumors abound that the barrier had been breached by human–monkey sexual activity in the jungle. More conservative medical opinion suggested careless handling of bushmeat kills by hunters was responsible. But hunters in Africa have been hunting and butchering chimpanzees and other Old World monkeys for thousands of years, so why would it have taken so long for SIV to make the jump?

In the recent past, medical opinion has been reappraised and is looking again at the HIV implications of the experiments of Ivanov and those of his equally misguided Russian contemporary, Serge Voronoff (see page 59).

BACK TO THE BEGINNING

One final word on the descent of man: For some time now, Africa has been regarded as the cradle of modern humanity. This notion moved from academic circles into the public consciousness in 2001 with the publication of Bryan Sykes's intriguing work of nonfiction *The Seven Daughters of Eve*. Sykes estimated that the first real human beings emerged in Central and Eastern Africa approximately 200,000 years ago.

But anthropologists will keep digging. In 2006, human teeth and countless animal bones bearing distinctive marks that indicate flesh had been stripped from them with flint implements were found in the Qesem Caves of Rosh Ha'Ayin, Israel. The remains were dated 200,000 years earlier than any African find. So unless Africa can come up with an earlier bid, the Holy Land holds the chalice—for the time being, at least.

African and Polynesian societies indulged in cannibalism.

The concept of cannibalism, that man could commit perhaps the ultimate crime of eating a fellow human being, has fascinated civilizations since ancient times. Hindu and Greek mythologies teem with examples of gods eating their own children, or vengeful wives serving up a favorite son in a stew to the unwitting and doting father. Today, people still tell the focus of their desires that they could eat them up, and there are numerous other edible metaphors for sex.

PAPAL TYRANNY

There was also in ancient times the well-established trend that required the devoted to sacrifice and devour a proxy for whichever god or demigod they worshiped. However, these would have been individual acts of anthrophagy (the eating of human flesh) conducted in a respectful and almost reverential way: the ingestion of blood and select body parts, such as the heart. Usually this was done to ensure the passage to heaven, or even rebirth, of the consumed. Although such concepts now seem primitive, today's Christians routinely partake in metaphorical anthrophagy: The wine-and-wafer ceremony of the Mass or Communion is thought to represent "the blood and body of Christ."

While there is a well-established history of such individual acts in ancient times, there has also existed a long-standing belief in the existence of countless African and Polynesian societies that indulged in routine anthrophagy as a staple part of their diet. Not challenged until the late twentieth century, this broadly accepted anthropological "truth" formed the basis of many expeditions that were usually followed by a highly lucrative lecture tour that brought the concept into the public awareness. Even today, no film of the *Indiana Jones* or *Lost World* genre is complete without at least one scene of someone being dropped into a pot on a low heat with suitably gruesome and bone-bedecked savages dancing around their dinner-to-be. And who is responsible for the spread of such ideas? The fifteenth-century Vatican and its avaricious rush to lay claim to the rest of the world.

THE AGE OF EXPLOITATION

During the Age of Exploration, from the fifteenth to the seventeenth centuries, the Catholic countries of Spain and Portugal stood at the helm of the discovery of the New World.

An illustration of the landing of Columbus

In addition to the gold and silver mined in these new lands, the profits to be made from slavery were enormous. Understandably, the Vatican felt in need of a veneer of justification for this slave trade, which itself presented a problem. Numerous popes and cardinals owned slaves, and the galleys of the papal navy ran on chained labor. But although the Bible abounded with divine justification of slavery of every kind, the Vatican was not anxious to make this known to the populations of Europe at large.

It must be remembered that this was a time when the Good Book was available only in Latin and any non-cleric who so much as peeked inside its covers could be burned alive for their curiosity. Anthrophagy, it seemed, presented the ideal solution. No indigenous peoples of new lands could be enslaved—we are all God's children, after all—unless they were found to be man-eaters, in which case they were not God's children but to be held lower than the beasts of the fields over which the Lord had given man dominion. Therefore man must have dominion over beings that ranked below beasts.

CANNIBALISM IS BORN

Before unleashing the rapacious Columbus on the unsuspecting peoples of foreign lands, Spain's Queen Isabella I of Castile and her husband, Ferdinand II of Aragon, sought clarification on the matter from Pope Alexander VI, a man not unaccustomed to employing a little brute force (see page 81). He was only too pleased to clarify, constructing the notorious Demarcation Line down the map of the world, with the Spanish to be kept to the west of it, and Portuguese to the east.

In 1492, Columbus duly headed for the Americas. Upon his arrival in the Caribbean, Columbus cynically pronounced the indigenous Canniba people to be wanton man-eaters and diligently set about their slaughter or enslavement. As this was the first major exercise of such a nature, the unfortunate natives' name gave rise to the term cannibal. Naturally, as soon as the explorers made landfall on a new country, they pronounced the entire population to be man-eaters and broke out the manacles, or worse. On Haiti alone, the Spanish reduced the indigenous Taino population from 500,000 to 350 people in a mere thirty years.

An artistic representation of Columbus's landing from a book dated 1891

*An early representation of
South American natives*

   To justify their preposterous claims, the enslaving expeditions published lurid pamphlets on their return, complete with etchings of trussed captives looking glum in their
cooking pots. These pamphlets would become standard
reference material for the early anthropologists of the eighteenth and nineteenth centuries, who set out in search of
suitably terrifying tribes. But their quests never quite came
to fruition—no single anthropologist ever visited a village
in which the occupants acknowledged themselves to be
cannibals.

THINGS DON'T ADD UP

It is extraordinary that these early anthropologists failed to ask basic questions that would have revealed the truth behind the fiction. How, for example, did Stone Age African or Polynesian tribesmen possess iron pots big enough to cook up the meat harvested from three or four victims? They also failed to work out the math: These were people who led an extremely harsh and active life without the comfort of an abundance of food. The average lithe native would produce up to ten pounds of meat at best, which would leave a village of one hundred adults requiring about ten victims for one decent meal. In the space of one year, the occupants of that one cannibalistic village would eat their way through something in the region of 4,000 of their neighbors—hardly a realistic prospect, given the population levels of such areas.

Anthropologists also failed to address the issues of practicality: The animals of the forests and the fishes of the rivers would have contributed a much higher meat yield, and they would not have shot back. Medical implications involved in eating one's fellow man would also have taken their toll. Eating humans is not good for you. Humans carry a dangerous prion, a protein particle thought to cause brain disease, similar to that which causes CJD, or "mad cow disease." The Fore tribe of Papua New Guinea, one of the few tribes known to conduct funeral cannibalistic rites, nearly wiped itself out in the late 1950s with a fatal condition similar to CJD, known locally as *kuru*, or the shaking death.

Anthropologists have certainly found ancient human bones bearing marks they claim were caused by butchery, but they cannot know the circumstances in which these injuries occurred. Starvation cannibalism is far from unknown in the apparently civilized West. The first English settlers of Jamestown, Virginia, resorted to eating one another when food supplies ran out in 1609; the Russians dined on one another in the Siege of Leningrad during World War II; and the diet of those who survived the Andean plane crash of 1972 is now common knowledge. Indeed, the vast majority of authenticated acts of cannibalism have involved white Europeans.

A PECKISH PACKER

The first prosecution for starvation cannibalism occurred in nineteenth-century America with the celebrated case of Alfred "Alferd" Packer (1842–1907). In November 1873, Packer foolishly led a party of gold prospectors from Gunnison, Colorado, up into the high country where, predictably, the weather trapped them in their shack. Packer soon realized that the only food he was going to find before the thaw set in would have to be provided, quite literally, by his clients. When Packer returned to Gunnison looking surprisingly well fed considering his ordeal, questions were asked . . . and the answers turned everyone pale.

Packer's subsequent trial is famous in America, not least for the presiding judge's summation. Judge Melville B. Gerry, a Democratic in the predominantly Republican state of Colorado, clearly felt a personal grudge against the defendant. Ordering Packer to stand for sentencing, Gerry said, "Damn you, Packer, there were only seven Democrats in the whole of Hinsdale County and you, you low-down son-of-a-bitch, ate five of them!"

The Earth is a hollow vessel.

Early religion touted the notion of a hollow Earth, a vessel that housed the "land of final punishment" for anyone who failed to conduct themselves in accordance with an individual religion's various dictates. For the Ancient Greeks hollow Earth was the Underworld, ruled by the god Hades, where all people, good or bad, ended up. For the Christians it was, and still is, the place we call Hell.

SCIENCE GETS INVOLVED

Inspired by theological pronouncements of an underground world, early science took the theory to heart and explored the concept. According to the proponents of the hollow Earth theory, our planet possessed a variety of characteristics, including an interior sun at its core, a living population, and access points at the Poles or in Tibet. Opinions on the exact details of the hollow Earth's makeup differed according to the sources.

In 1692, Edmond Halley (1656–1742), the astronomer and polymath of comet fame, advanced a theory that suggested the planet was a hollow shell that contained three inner shells. He believed each independent and inhabited sphere was separated from its neighboring sphere by its own atmosphere. The access points to the interior of the earth were, according to Halley, located at the Poles, and gases escaping from within the earth manifested themselves as the aurora borealis. Halley's hypothesis drew considerable recognition.

It was Halley's 1676 voyage to St. Helena to observe the star constellations in the southern hemisphere that started him thinking seriously about the ancient hollow Earth theory. He was struck by the inconsistencies in his compass

REALITY CHECK
TURNING UP THE HEAT

Mark Twain once remarked, "Heaven for the climate, but Hell for the company" but, according to the Bible, Heaven is the hotter of the two. Isaiah 30:26 describes that in Heaven "the light of the sun shall be sevenfold as the light of seven days," which, according to a series of weighty calculations involving the Stefan–Boltzmann fourth power law of radiation, gives us a temperature of 977° Fahrenheit (525° Celsius). Hell, the Bible tells us, abounds with pits of liquid brimstone (sulfur), so the temperature there must be 833° Fahrenheit (445 degrees Celsius), because any temperature higher than that turns sulfur into gas.

The hollow earth with access points at both Poles

readings, which seemed to vary even on the same spot on consecutive days. What else would account for this except another rotating sphere, or two, within the casing of the planet? Of course, what Halley did not then know was that this discrepancy in compass readings is quite normal: The lines of the Earth's magnetic field do not run in straight lines between the Poles, but in a series of erratic lines, which themselves shift.

The idea that the lines of the Earth's magnetic field were caused by something deep within the Earth was the thrust of the first part of Halley's 1692 submission to the Royal Society. If one allowed for the notion of other spheres that possessed their own magnetic fields, which rotate at different speeds or even in different directions, then this would account for the varying compass readings. Halley informed the assembled members of the Royal Society that

REALITY CHECK
THE UNRELIABLE COMPASS

The old-fashioned needle compass aligns itself with whichever line is nearest and thus never points to true North, unless by pure coincidence. The lines are generated by the rotating, solid iron ball at the center of the planet, which is, at present, behaving in a rather worrying way. Things, it seems, are afoot beneath our feet, and some feel the Earth is preparing for a reversal of its own polarization. This change happens approximately every 250,000 years, and we are long overdue such an upheaval.

his notions fitted with the theological perspective that the Almighty would not, in His wisdom, have created the massive bulk of the world "simply to support its surface" but instead "to yield as great a surface as possible for the use of living creatures as can consist with the convenience and security of the whole." When asked why the oceans did not drain away into the hollow after sub-oceanic earthquakes tore open cracks in the Earth's surface, Halley's answer was that the outer sphere, perhaps 500 miles thick, was obviously self-healing due to the presence of "saline and vitriolic particles as may contribute to petrification."

Halley concluded his submission by saying that "The concave arches may in several places shine with such a substance as invests the surface of the Sun and I have adventured to make these subterranean orbs capable of being inhabited." From those last few words on the subject there sprang a whole new interest in hollow-earthism.

DEARLY DEVOTED

The list of those who took Halley at his tantalizing word is long to say the least, but among the more prominent were the Norwegian-born essayist and philosopher Ludvig Holberg (1684–1754), who enshrined his ideas in the novel *The Journey of Niels Klim to the World Underground* (1741). In a yarn that would long predate Jules Verne's altogether more enjoyable *Journey to the Center of the Earth* (1863), Holberg's fantasy tells the story of a young student who discovers a series of worlds within our own after falling into a cave. His exciting journey leads him to explore new lands and strange creatures that live under the earth's crust.

The eighteenth-century hollow-earthers also counted among its ranks the Scottish mathematician and physicist Sir John Leslie (1776–1832). In his *Elements of Natural Philosophy* (1829) he devotes nearly half a dozen pages to the concept. In the nineteenth century the leading lights of the lobby were the Americans John Cleves Symmes (1779–1829), James McBride (1788–1859), and Jeremiah Reynolds (1799–1858). The first is best described as a well-connected adventurer, McBride was a leading light of Miami University, and

Reynolds a well-respected newspaper editor and explorer.

Together the three men lobbied President John Quincy Adams (1767–1848), who, as a proponent of the hollow Earth theory, agreed to fund from the public purse an expedition to the South Pole to find the portal to the supposed subterranean wonders. However, the project was abandoned when Adams's replacement, the altogether more hard-headed Andrew Jackson (1767–1845), threw the idea and its proponents out on their collective ear.

Undeterred, Reynolds immediately raised funds for the expedition from private backers and speculators, and set sail in late 1929 in search of his goal. His crew, however, were unconvinced, and having quickly tired of looking for a big hole in the earth's surface under the supervision of a man they thought was crazy, they mutinied and set Reynolds ashore on the coast of Chile before sailing off in his ship. Reynolds was forced to wait in Valparaiso until 1932, when he was eventually rescued by an American ship.

NAZI INVOLVEMENT

Not one to let a dubious scientific theory pass by unnoticed, Adolf Hitler too propagated the theory of a hollow Earth. The Thule Society, a large collection of right-wing eccentrics who adhered to all sorts of mystical notions, provided the hub of support in Germany. It was from this semi-clandestine society that the Nazi Party itself sprang. The Thulians believed the access to the inner world lay in Tibet, a country they also believed to be the cradle of a long-lost master race — Hitler and a majority of his henchmen also believed this to be true.

In 1938, Hitler and Heinrich Himmler sent an expedition to Tibet to find anthropological evidence of the supposed master race and, while they were there, to investigate any suspiciously large holes they might happen to encounter. The expedition heard much talk of the fabled underworld cities of Agartha and Shambhala (now known as "Shangri-La" to Westerners) and the superior beings who lived there. Despite the explorers leaving their first expedition empty-handed, Hitler had not yet finished with the Underworld. In 1943 the Führer decided it was time he explored the other hollow earth theory: the earth is a concave sphere and all living creatures inhabit its inside surface.

In April 1942, Hitler sent an expedition under the leadership of Dr. Heinz Fischer to Rügen Island, located in the Baltic Sea, where they set up camp with powerful telescopes and radar. They were under instruction to aim their instruments up at the sky, rather than across the sea, to spy on Allied activity on the other side of the world. Unsurprisingly, the members of the expedition returned to Berlin in late May empty-handed and no doubt fearful of reprisal from their dogmatic leader. Fortunately for them, the high-ranking Nazi Reinhard Heydrich had recently been assassinated in Czechoslovakia, and Hitler was far more interested in plotting his revenge. Relieved, Fischer took himself off to secure obscurity and all further Nazi-led hollow Earth projects were abandoned. But the theory of a hollow Earth did not die out with Hitler. There remain today countless hollow Earth societies, all of which, of course, believe that the successes of the various NASA-led space programs are but a charade to keep us from communicating with our inner selves.

The bodies of animals contain a life energy that can be influenced by external magnetic forces.

To suggest someone possesses an animal magnetism is to imply they are sexually attractive or have a charismatic allure, but the original meaning of the expression suggested nothing of the kind. First realized in the eighteenth century, animal magnetism was a new "science" that suggested people and animals possessed a universal fluid that could be influenced by an external magnetic force. This notion held sway for some considerable time, and would go on to spawn the phenomenon of hypnotism.

ANIMAL MAGNETISM

Austrian-born Franz Anton Mesmer (1734–1815), a physician with an interest in astronomy, first devised the concept of animal magnetism, and he did so under the tutelage of

the incongruously named Jesuit astronomer Father Maximilian Hell (1720–92).

Aside from his interest in the universe, Maximilian Hell
also had a keen interest in the spurious field of magnetic
therapy, born in part from his familiarity with the Chinese
concept of qi (pronounced "chee"). This notion centered on
the ancient oriental belief that certain vital energies flow
through the body and that the disruption of these energies
can lead to bad health. Wellness is reestablished by redirecting the flow of qi using a variety of techniques, from
feng shui to acupuncture and magnet therapy.

The acupuncture needles and magnets were intended to
act like corporeal traffic police by redirecting the energy
flow to its correct route. Hell had no time for acupuncture;
he was convinced the magnets, rather than the needles, held
the key to the cure. Hell started to build medicinal magnet
theory into his lectures, and his student Mesmer joined him
wholeheartedly in his folly.

Mesmer was also greatly influenced by the British royal
physician Richard Mead (1673–1754), the "Father of Found-
lings," whose spacious residence in Bloomsbury, London,
would form the foundation of the Great Ormond Street Hospital for Sick Children. Mead had a keen interest in astronomy and—after his close friend Isaac Newton discovered the
universal force of gravity—postulated that just as the planets
exerted a gravitational pull on the Earth, they similarly influenced the flow of fluids within animals and humans.

While the gravitational pull of the moon creates tides in the Earth's oceans, for example, the human body is far too small an object to be subjected to similar effects. Mesmer, however, used the false postulations of Hell and Mead to devise the concept of animal gravitation.

Mesmer next observed the Bavarian priest exorcist Johann Gassner (1727–79) during a routine exorcism. Mesmer concluded that the patient's possession was alleviated by the magnetism that emitted from a metal cross the priest had used to beat and stroke the afflicted. In the belief that there might be an interaction between a natural magnetic quality within the body and the external magnetic force, Mesmer devised the concept of animal magnetism.

Mesmer was convinced that a universal fluid, a force that flowed like liquid through all living creatures, could be manipulated by an external magnetic influence. In order to test his hypothesis, Mesmer subjected his patients to a variety of bizarre treatments, one of which included having them sit in a vat of diluted sulfuric acid while they held on to iron bars that carried a low-voltage current.

MESMERISM

By 1775 Mesmer abandoned the use of magnets and electricity altogether, as he had become convinced that he himself was the vector directing and controlling the ebb and flow of a person's universal fluid. By this stage his patients

REALITY CHECK
THE INFLUENCE OF THE MOON

Planetary influence on the well-being of humankind was not in itself a new notion. The word *lunatic*, derived from the Latin *luna* (moon), suggested the full moon could induce abnormal behavior in those who were normally sane. In the days before street lighting there may have been some foundation in such a notion. Taking advantage of the free light provided by the full moon, people might well have stayed out longer, allowing them the opportunity to drink more than usual. Or perhaps they always behaved like that and it was just that their transgressions were more visible to sober observers.

were required to sit in mesmeric cubicles, which, they were told, would concentrate "the force" on them.

Nor was Mesmer alone in his beliefs—many physicians of significant standing followed his teachings, and "mesmerism" became popular throughout eighteenth-century Europe. In Mesmer's defense, his research did lead to a groundbreaking discovery; unfortunately he was too enamored with the notion of animal magnetism to acknowledge the phenomenon for what it really was.

Mesmer enjoyed some considerable success in his sessions, which had become a cross between a pseudoscience and spiritual healing. His success, however, may have been

Franz Anton Mesmer at work

the result of his propensity to focus his attentions on hypochondriacs, hysterics, and those otherwise susceptible to his suggestions. The most celebrated of such patients was the talented pianist Maria Theresia von Paradis (1759–1824), whose father was prominent in the Austrian court and held the ear of the Empress Maria Theresa, after whom he had named his daughter.

Having suffered from "hysterical blindness" since the age of four, the eighteen-year-old Maria Theresia expe-

rienced a temporary improvement in her sight under the
guidance of Mesmer. But when it was suggested that Mesmer had used his influence over Maria Theresia to put her
into one of his famous mesmeric trances for other, less salu-
brious purposes, her parents felt they had no option but to
dispense with his services. As soon as the treatments were
terminated the blindness returned and remained with Maria Theresia for the rest of her life.

This illustration adorns the frontispiece of
Confessions of a Magnetizer,
an 1845 exposé of animal magnetism.

The whiff of scandal was enough to force Mesmer to quit Vienna and head to Paris, where he continued his lucrative practice. Mesmer began to record that the influence he communicated to his patients induced what he called a magnetic trance, or magnetic somnambulance. Although he did not realize it, Mesmer was hypnotizing his patients.

MESMER IS MARGINALIZED

As Mesmer's bandwagon picked up momentum in France, Louis XVI came under increasing pressure to establish a scientific inquiry into the matter. Despite being one of Mesmer's patients, Louis XVI finally gave the green light in 1784 for a Commission. One of the members of the committee was Dr. Joseph-Ignace Guillotin, an expert in pain management whose name would soon be made infamous by the impending French Revolution.

Guillotin and his cocommittee members found no merit in Mesmer's methods or treatments, and they denounced him as a fraud. Another prominent name on the committee, Benjamin Franklin (1706–90), one of the Founding Fathers of the United States, then in Paris as the United States Minister to France, concurred, although he did add that Mesmer clearly had an idea of the role the mind played in sickness and its cure.

HYPNOTIC

As Mesmer became increasingly marginalized, one of his French students, José Faria (1746–1819), an Indo-Portuguese monk from Goa, began to incorporate the techniques used in oriental hypnotism into the sessions. The results were revelatory. Finally realizing that hypnotism, and not animal magnetism, lay at the heart of Mesmer's sessions, Faria pronounced that "Nothing comes from the magnetizer: everything comes from the subject and takes place in his imagination; [it is] autosuggestion generated from within the mind [of the subject]."

Faria's take on the matter would outlive him. His methods were later observed by the English physician James Braid (1795–1860), who in 1841 made a close study of this modified form of mesmerism and refined it to become the first modern clinical hypnotism, a term he coined himself.

With this new life breathed into the phenomenon of mesmerism, others sought to apply the concept to the rest of the animal kingdom. The methods employed by North African and Indian snake charmers were reevaluated—was it just a street trick, or did something more sophisticated occur between the charmer and the charmed? Chickens, too, seemed to fall into a trance if held down against the ground as a chalk line was drawn away from the tip of their beak.

Unfortunately for those who like to believe in such things, animals cannot be mesmerized or hypnotized. The snake-charming acts are nothing but a street trick; the music from the charmer's flute is quite unnecessary to the ruse, as its pitch lies outside of a snake's auditory range. (It is a myth too that snakes are deaf—they simply do not have external ears, only internal ones that pick up vibration

A chicken undergoing hypnosis

through the ground.) The key to the trick is the tapping of the charmer's foot and the movement of his flute.

The strike distance of a cobra is approximately two-thirds of its body length, and the creature has motion-sensitive vision. The foundation to a long career as a snake charmer lies in their ability to position themselves just outside of that range, but not so far that the snake loses interest and slides back down into its basket. The snake appears to mimic the flute's movement from side to side, as if in a trance; in reality it is preparing itself to strike the charmer, should the opportunity present itself.

Chickens, on the other hand, go into a state of thanatosis (feigned death), in response to the sheer fear they experience at being held immobile, as if in the grip of a predator. The carefully drawn chalk line is a mere piece of theatre, unnecessary to the procedure.

THE LEGACY LIVES ON

While mesmerism finally waned, and its offspring, hypnotism, went on to achieve greater things, certain charlatans were not yet done with magnet therapy. There still exists today a multimillion-dollar industry that peddles magnetic bangles to the gullible, promising improved blood flow and relief from pain in the wrists and hands. An Internet search for "magnetic bracelets" renders nearly 2 million sites.

Nor has Mesmer's original idea of a universal force

that flows through the bodies of all animals been completely disregarded. For some, *orgone*, a so-called cosmic energy discovered by the Austrian-born psychiatrist and psychoanalyst Wilhelm Reich (1897–1957), held the key. For others it was, and still is for some, *vril*, a powerful life-giving and life-destroying force first introduced in Edward Bulwer-Lytton's 1871 novel *The Coming Race*, which some took to be a fictionalized realization of a very real force. Mesmer's ideas even form the foundation of the Star Wars franchise, in which the Force is always with those willing to recognize and harness it.

A close friend of Sigmund Freud and a member of the so-called Vienna Circle, Reich was captivated by Freud's notion of libido. For Reich libido was the universal force, which he chose to call *orgone* (a blend of *orgasm* and *ozone*). Under the pretense that he could tap into the vibrations of an enduring cosmic orgasm, Reich built orgone accumulators, largely modeled on the mesmeric cubicles and into which he invited his human guinea pigs for a quick blast of celestial sex-energy. Reich's accumulator was essentially a Faraday cage (invented in 1836 by the English scientist Michael Faraday for the use in blocking external electric fields), insulated on the outside by wood and lined on the inside with thin steel sheeting. He believed the orgone accumulator contained concentrated orgone energy that could be used to cure illness in those who were experiencing an imbalance in their orgone.

Participants emerged claiming to feel suitably invigo-
rated, however Reich did select his volunteers from a circle
of the already converted. Interestingly, Reich did attract
some notable names to his camp—even Albert Einstein
(1879–1955) thought there might be something in it. After
a five-hour meeting between the two men at Princeton University in January 1941, Einstein declared that if Reich's
experiments revealed a detectable rise in temperature in
one of his accumulators without a known heat source, then
the basic laws of physics would have been discredited.

Reich returned to Princeton with an accumulator so Einstein could observe for himself the increase in temperature.
And observe it he did. Einstein's experiments revealed a
noticeable increase in the internal temperature of the accumulator; however, this increase was detectable only in
the upper section of the box, and it was soon established
the temperature change was the consequence of convection
currents from the room itself and not the result of a cosmic
influence.

The accumulators were not airtight; the only thing they
did accumulate was warm air from without. In 1954 the US
Food and Drug Administration (FDA) issued Reich with
an injunction, banning him from selling or transporting his
accumulators. But Reich was by then a psychotic paranoid
with delusions of grandeur, and he chose to ignore the writ.
He ended his days in a psychiatric prison, a somewhat dis-
graced figure. Reich's accumulators are still available to

MINI MYTHS
WELL, I NEVER!
POPULAR SCIENTIFIC IDEAS DEBUNKED

- Water does not spiral down the drain in different directions in the northern and southern hemispheres.
- Goldfish have pretty good memories and can even be taught a trick or two!
- Black holes do not absorb surrounding matter.
- Electricity actually flows from negative to positive.
- The Big Bang Theory relates to the early evolution of the universe, not its inception.

buy online for a mere $5,000, which the unkind might say is a touch steep for what is essentially a steel-lined coffin. But many are willing to pay such sums to be at one with the universe.

THE NEXT GENERATION

Bulwer-Lytton's vril was perhaps mesmerism's most sinister spin-off. *The Coming Race* combined the notion of a hollow Earth (see page 147) with the universal force of mesmerism. For Bulwer-Lytton, vril flowed like a magical fluid through the bodies of a subterranean superrace that was biding its time for a terrestrial takeover. Such was the international popularity of this yarn it even inspired product names such as Bovril—a blend of *bovine* and *vril*.

The Coming Race was a great hit in Germany, especially among certain societies that had started to emerge in the early 1900s. The Thule Society in particular thought the book was fact masquerading as fiction. The Thulians believed the Earth was a hollow vessel, within which dwelled the mythical Aryan race, biding its time before bursting forth on to the Earth's surface to take over the world.

From the Thulian membership would emerge the Nazi Party (see page 152). Under the guiding hand of Himmler, in 1935 Hitler set up the *Studiengesellschaft für Geistergeschichte, Deutsches Ahnenerbe* (the Study Society for Spiritual History and German Ancestral Heritage), which was charged with proving the existence of a subterranean superrace. Their mission was to establish contact and reassure the subterranean dwellers that they had allies on the surface who would be there to support them when the time came.

This was the hidden agendum of the infamous 1938 German expedition to Tibet, as led by SS member and German hunter Ernst Schäfer (1910–92) and his Deputy Expedition Leader, fellow SS member Bruno Berger (1911–2009). The official reason given for the expedition was to research the geography and culture of the region, but Berger and his SS colleagues did little more than take cranial measurements of the local people and make phrenological head casts with the results.

The last word on the subject of animal magnetism is awarded to Willy Ley (1906–69), the leading rocket scientist who had the good sense to leave Germany in 1935. In 1947 Ley wrote an article called "Pseudoscience in Naziland" in which he mentioned a sub-group of the Thule Society that was exclusively founded on the contents of Bulwer-Lytton's *The Coming Race*.

"The next group was literally founded upon a novel," wrote Ley. "That group, which I think called itself *Wahrheitsgesellschaft* (the Society for Truth) and which was more or less localized in Berlin, devoted its spare time looking for vril." Indeed there still exist vril societies throughout Europe and North America today. Perhaps someone should tell them it was all just a story.

The body is made up of four humors—blood, phlegm, yellow bile, and black bile.

From Ancient Greece to the mid- to late nineteenth century, the "humor theory"—the idea that the body is made up of four main fluids—was a broadly accepted phenomenon.

Consisting of blood, phlegm, yellow bile, and black bile, an imbalance in the four humors was said to cause all sickness and mental malaise. Too much phlegm and a person would become phlegmatic; an excess of blood (or *sanguis*) was thought to make a person sanguine; too much yellow bile (or *chole*) would likely induce cholera; and too much black bile (or *melanchole*) and a person would sink into a melancholy mood. These four basic concepts constituted a comprehensive framework of health and disease made available to doctors until it was superseded by scientific medicine in the nineteenth century.

This engraving dates from the sixteenth century and shows the perceived balance of the four humors

FOUNDATION STONES

The foundation for the humor theory lay in Hippocratic medicine. Beginning with the Ancient Greek medic Hippocrates (c. 460–c. 370 BCE) and developed by unknown individuals over the course of next two centuries, the Hippocratic Corpus was later introduced to the West by the physician, surgeon, and pivotal figure in Greek medicine Galen (129–c. 210 CE). The theory held that each of the four humors was identified with a body part and linked to one of the four elements—phlegm was matched with the brain and water, blood with the heart and air, black bile with the spleen and the Earth, and yellow bile with the liver and fire. The properties of the four humors were heat, cold, dryness, and moistness.

The Hippocratic approach was holistic—the ancient Greeks knew little about the human anatomy, as they were averse to dissecting human bodies; they favored instead a surface inspection of their patients to see if they could spot the likely signs of disease. Physicians believed they could read the complex balance of the four humors in an individual's face, hence *complexion*. The cosmetics trade was in part put into hyperdrive by the humor theory, as both men and women tried to present to the world a visage that spoke well of their physical and mental disposition. The multibillion-dollar industry thus has the Greeks to thank for its existence. As the theory expanded, it embraced the notion that you are what you eat. Foods were categorized according to the effect they had on the humors, and this shaped the different cooking styles of medieval Europe.

MINI MYTH
FOOD, GLORIOUS FOOD

The different nations of medieval Europe each had a slightly different take on how food might influence a person's humoral balance. Red meat was thought to anger the blood, but if cooked in honey the effect would be reduced. An imbalance in bile could be treated with foods dressed in saffron. Not only did the humor theory invade the medieval kitchen, the chefs themselves rose to physician-like status, commanding considerable pay and respect.

BLOODY EXCESS

Proponents of the four humors believed the body could heal itself, and their procedures were designed to encourage the body in this natural healing process by purging it of its bad humors. Bloodletting was a common practice, often carried out to help alleviate fever and to remove excess blood, and it continued well into the mid-nineteenth century. So popular was bloodletting that, no matter their condition, many patients were bled relentlessly by their doctors, often with terminal results. President George Washington (1731–99), British poet Lord Byron (1788–1024), and the Scottish poet and playwright Sir Walter

Scott (1771–1832) all died as a result of bloodletting by well-intentioned doctors.

The notion that humoral bleeding improved a person's outlook was so popular that even barbers would help patients dispense with a pint or two. In the fourteenth century the Worshipful Company of Barbers and Surgeons was established to enable barbers to come to the aid of monks, who

There will be blood: a lithograph from 1804

MINI MYTH
LINGUISTIC LEGACY

Adherents to the humor theory thought the liver, and not the heart, was the seat of courage. The heart was believed to be the home of learning, hence to "learn something by heart." The liver was thought to house a reservoir of yellow bile, which supposedly deserted the organ in times of stress, hence the cowardly are sometimes said to be either "lily livered" or "yellow bellied."

at that time were the official practitioners of medicine but who were banned from spilling blood by papal decree. The company was eventually dissolved in 1745 when the surgeons broke away to form the Company of Surgeons, yet its legacy can still be seen in the barber's pole today: The brass cap represents the collection bowl, and the red-and-white stripes the blood seeping through the bandaged incision.

FOUNDATION STONE

Hippocratic medicine highlighted the role the brain played in influencing a person's emotions, an idea previously unfamiliar within Ancient Greece, where it was believed the heart was responsible for a person's mental functions. Humorists believed mental health was dictated by the humoral

A look says it all: the faces of the four humors.
(Clockwise from top) phlegmatic, sanguine,
melancholic, and choleric

balance, which provided the foundations for modern psychology. To *temper* something is to mix or blend, and the right blend of the humors was believed to engender a good *temperament*. To the proto-psychologist there were four main temperaments, each dictated by the four cardinal humors. The sanguine were believed to be impulsive and extroverted yet also lofty and prone to taking delight in being hurtful to those near to them. The choleric were aggressive control freaks who did well in the world of politics. The phlegmatic were passive-aggressive types who made good followers. And the melancholic, well, they spoke for themselves. While these beliefs were very broad, this was the start of a scientific understanding of what went on in the minds of those in a distracted or depressed state.

The alternative practice of homeopathy also has its roots in the humor theory. Distressed at the bloodletting, leeching, purging, and other undignified and potentially terminal procedures that were being carried out, the German-born physician Christian Samuel Friedrich Hahnemann (1755–1843) investigated alternative procedures. Rather than letting fluids out of the body, Hahnemann pondered, why not impose a balance in the humors by more subtle means? He published his ideas in *The Organon of Homeopathic Medicine* (1810).

Doubtless influenced by the principles of inoculation and vaccination, as developed by the general practitioner

Edward Jenner (1749–1823), Hahnemann focused on the concept of fighting like with like. He suggested that treatment of a medical condition should consist of administering a very dilute dose of substances that, in larger doses, would produce the symptoms that had initially ailed the patient. Interestingly, in Greek, *homeo* translates as "the same," and *pathos* means "suffering." Unfortunately Hahnemann took his idea to an extreme, and began speaking of magical dilutions that, when shaken by the practitioner, would release "immaterial and spiritual power." He believed that with a simple tap of the bottled dilution on the heel of the hand, the practitioner could "double the dilution" of the medicine, that is half the strength yet again, and thus greatly increase its curative power.

Aside from Hahnemann's somewhat illogical notion that the weaker the dose, the more powerful the cure, homeopaths also believed that water possessed a memory of anything it might come into contact with, so a substance diluted to the point of virtual nonexistence would be the most powerful of all. Many modern homeopathists still believe this to be true, but let us hope they have been misled, otherwise our planet's water, which has been subjected to all manner of chemicals and fecal matter over the centuries, would surely be the most toxic substance known to man. Despite the far-out nature of some of Hahnemann's theories, he deserves to be held in fond memory for having saved many a patient from being drained of blood at a time when they needed it most.

As for Hahnemann's principles of dilution: I have conducted my own tests with whiskey and, cross my heart, I can affirm that one drop of single malt in a glass of water will not blow you out of your chair. It is far more effective to drink it neat.

BIBLIOGRAPHY

∽⚬∾

Berry, Adrian. *Eureka!* London: Harrap Books, 1989.

Boese, Alex. *Elephants on Acid and Other Bizarre Experiments.* London: Pan Books, 2009.

Bynum, William F. *Science and the Practice of Medicine in the Nineteenth Century.* Cambridge: Cambridge University Press, 1994.

— — —. *The History of Medicine: A Very Short Introduction.* Oxford: Oxford University Press, 2008.

Carroll, Robert Todd. *The Skeptic's Dictionary.* Hoboken, NJ: John Wiley & Sons, 2003.

Friedman, Stanton T., and Kathleen Marden. *Science Was Wrong.* Pompton Plains, NJ: Career Press, 2010.

Goldacre, Ben. *Bad Science.* London: Harper Perennial, 2009.

Lilienfeld, Scott O., Steven Jay Lynn, John Ruscio, and Barry L. Beyerstein. *50 Great Myths of Popular Psychology.* West Sussex, UK: Wiley-Blackwell, 2010.

Plait, Philip C. *Bad Astronomy.* Hoboken, NJ: John Wiley & Sons, 2002.

Pollard, Justin. *Boffinology.* London: John Murray Publishers, 2010.

Porter, Roy. *The Greatest Benefit to Mankind.* New York: HarperCollins, 1997.

Schneider, Reto U. *The Mad Science Book.* London: Quercus, 2008.

Singh, Simon, and Edzard Ernst. *Trick or Treatment.* London: Corgi Books, 2009.

Wanjek, Christopher. *Bad Medicine.* Hoboken, NJ: John Wiley & Sons, 2002.

INDEX

∽∘∾

Note: Page numbers in *italic* refer to illustrations.

Credits and Acknowledgments

Pages 31 and 35: www.karenswhimsy.com/
public-domain-images.

Page 55: Mary Evans Picture Library/Interfoto Agentur.

Page 57: © Science Museum/Science & Society Picture Library
(all rights reserved).

Page 65: Library of Congress (LC-DIG-ppmsca-27955).

Page 71: © The Art Archive/Alamy.

Pages 84 and 124: www.clipart.com.

Page 87: Walter Daran/Time & Life Pictures/Getty Images.

Page 112: Courtesy of Institute for Nearly Genius Research,
www.bonkersinstitute.org.

Page 118: Interfoto/ Sammlung Rauch/Mary Evans Picture
Library.

Page 122: Miles Kelly/fotoLibra.

ALSO AVAILABLE FROM READER'S DIGEST

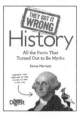

They Got It Wrong: History

They Got It Wrong: History exposes historical fallacies from the Roman Empire to World War II. Separate out the facts from shadowy fictions and illuminate how and why these falsehoods got passed around as truths.

Emma Marriott
ISBN 978-1-62145-008-5 • $15.99 hardcover

Bible Stories You May Have Forgotten: Miracles, Adventures and Life Lessons from Genesis to Revelation

Does the Tower of Babel ring a bell, or do you need to clean the cobwebs out of your belfry? This light and witty reference book gives readers the basics of all the stories they need to know, condensed for ease of understanding and entertainment.

James Stuart Bell and Sam O'Neal
ISBN 978-1-62145-003-0 • $14.99 hardcover

Quotable Quotes: All New Wit & Wisdom from the Greatest Minds of Our Time

The most well-known and succinct personalities of our time lend their memorable pearls of wit and wisdom—from comedians to scientists, from presidents to performers, from authors to athletes—to this updated edition of the best-selling book.

ISBN 978-1-62145-004-7 • $14.99 hardcover

The Insult Dictionary: History's Best Slights, Street Talk, and Slang

Do you long for the days when a jerk was a "cad"? Want to tell that "swillbelly" to clean up his table manners and that grumbling "glump" to stop whining? All this churlishness and more can be found in the pages of this complete(ly hilarious) guide to waxing vintage.

Julie Tibbott
ISBN 978-1-62145-066-5 • $14.99 hardcover

For more information, visit us at RDTradePublishing.com
E-book editions are also available.

Reader's Digest books can be purchased through retail and online bookstores.
In the United States books are distributed by Penguin Group (USA), Inc.
For more information or to order books, call 1-800-788-6262.

There is a missing link in the evolutionary chain.

Cocaine and heroin can cure a range of man's ills.

The physical measurements of the skull correlate to a person's personality.

The body is made up of four humors—blood, phlegm, yellow bile, and black bile.

Disease is caused by foul smell and lack of personal hygiene.

A battalion of marching soldiers can cause a suspension bridge to collapse.

The Earth is a hollow vessel.

The bodies of animals contain a life energy that can be influenced by external magnetic forces.